ENGLISH SHORT STORIES FOR INTERMEDIATE LEARNERS

EIGHT UNCONVENTIONAL SHORT STORIES TO GROW YOUR VOCABULARY AND LEARN ENGLISH THE FUN WAY!

OLLY RICHARDS

Olly Richards Publishing

olly@iwillteachyoualanguage.com

Trademarked names appear throughout this book. Rather than use a trademark symbol with every occurrence of a trademarked name, names are used in an editorial fashion with no intention of infringement of the respective owner's trademark.

The information in this book is distributed on an "as is" basis without warranty. Although every precaution has been taken in the preparation of this work, neither the author nor the publisher shall have any liability to any person or entity with respect to any loss or damage caused or alleged to be caused directly or indirectly by the information contained in this book.

English Short Stories for Intermediate Learners: *Eight Unconventional Short Stories to Grow Your Vocabulary and Learn English the Fun Way!*

ISBN- 978-1533319449

ISBN- 1533319448

Free Masterclass:
How To Read Effectively In A Foreign Language

As a special thank you for investing in this book, I invite you to attend a FREE online workshop. You'll learn how to read effectively, so you can understand more, and improve your English faster.

To register for the workshop, visit:

http://iwillteachyoualanguage.com/readingmasterclass

Books in this Series

Spanish Short Stories For Beginners
Spanish Short Stories For Beginners Volume 2
German Short Stories For Beginners
Italian Short Stories For Beginners
Italian Short Stories For Beginners Volume 2
Russian Short Stories For Beginners
French Short Stories For Beginners

English Short Stories For Intermediate Learners
Spanish Short Stories For Intermediate Learners
Italian Short Stories For Intermediate Learners

Many of these titles are also available as audiobooks

For more information visit:
http://iwillteachyoualanguage.com/amazon

Introduction

This book is a collection of eight entertaining short stories in English. The stories are written for intermediate learners, equivalent to B1-B2 on the Common European Framework of Reference (CEFR). They are a fun and effective way to improve your English and grow your vocabulary.

Reading is one of the best ways to improve your English, but it can be difficult to find suitable reading material. Many books are difficult to understand. They contain advanced vocabulary, and are so long you can feel overwhelmed and want to give up.

If you recognise these problems, then this book is for you. There are many kinds of stories in the book, such as science fiction, fantasy, thriller, and crime. As you begin to read, you will forget that you are reading in a foreign language, and enjoy discovering different worlds in English!

There are many useful features in the book that help you read more effectively. For example, after each chapter there is a summary of the plot and a set of comprehension questions, so you can check important details of the story. You will learn a lot of natural English and improve quickly.

As an intermediate learner of English, you might be looking for an entertaining challenge. Or maybe, you have been learning for a while and simply want to enjoy reading. Either way, this book is the biggest step forward you will take in your English this year.

So, sit back and relax. It's time to let your imagination run wild and enter a magical English world of fun, mystery, and intrigue!

Table of Contents

About the Stories

A feeling of progress is important when reading in a foreign language. Without this, you have no motivation to keep reading. The stories in *English Short Stories for Intermediate Learners* have been designed to give you this feeling of progress.

First, each story has been kept short and broken down into chapters. This gives you the satisfaction of being able to finish reading what you have started, and come back the next day wanting more. It also reduces the feeling of: "There is so much I don't know in English!"

The English in the stories is rich and varied, but still understandable for intermediate learners. Each story is written in a different genre in order to keep you entertained. There are plenty of dialogues, giving you lots of useful spoken English words and phrases to learn. There is also a variety of tenses from one story to the next, so you can practise common verbs in past, present, and future forms. This will make you a more confident user of English, able to understand different situations without getting lost.

English Short Stories for Intermediate Learners supports you with some special learning features. There are regular summaries of the plot to help you follow the story and make sure you have not missed anything important. You will find comprehension questions at the end of each chapter to test your understanding of what has happened in the story and encourage you to read in more detail.

English Short Stories for Intermediate Learners has been created to give you the support you need, so you can focus on reading, learning, and having fun!

How to Read Effectively

Reading is an important skill, and in our mother tongue, we read in different ways. For example, we might *skim* a news article quickly in order to understand the main events. Or, we might *scan* the pages of a bus timetable looking for a particular time or place. If I gave you a children's book to read, you would turn the pages quickly. On the other hand, if I gave you a contract to sign, you would read each word carefully.

However, when it comes to reading in a foreign language, research tells us that we lose most of our reading skills. We stop using skills like skimming and scanning to help us understand difficult texts. Instead, we simply start at the beginning and read every word, one after the other. Inevitably, we quickly become frustrated by difficult words.

As long as you are aware of this, however, you can use some simple strategies to avoid this trap and become a better reader.

* * *

You are reading this book because you like the idea of learning English with short stories. But why? What are the benefits of learning English with stories, instead of with a textbook? Understanding this will help you improve your reading.

When you read books for fun, it is known as *extensive reading*. This is very different from how you might read English in a textbook. Your textbook contains short dialogues, which you read in detail. The aim is to understand every word. This is known as *intensive reading*.

Here is another way to look at it. Textbooks give you grammar rules and lists of vocabulary to learn; they try to teach you. Stories show you "real English"; they do not try to teach you. In fact, both kinds of reading are valuable and you need them both in order to learn a language effectively.

English Short Stories for Intermediate Learners, however, is designed to help you with extensive reading. As you read and enjoy the stories, you will gradually improve your understanding of how English works. If you often study with textbooks, this book will be a breath of fresh air!

Now, in order to get the benefits of extensive reading, you have to make sure you are reading regularly. Reading one or two pages may teach you a few new words, but it will not make a big difference to the level of your English. With this in mind, here is what you should have in mind when you read the stories in this book, so you learn the most from them:

1. There are two things that are vital to successful reading: enjoyment, and a sense of achievement. They are important because they make you want to come back the next day and read more.
2. The more you read, the more you learn.
3. The best way to enjoy reading stories, and to feel a sense of achievement, is by reading the story from beginning to end.
4. Consequently, understanding every word in a story is *not* the most important thing. The most important thing is reaching the end of the story.

This brings us to the most important point of this section: **You must accept that you will not understand everything you read in a story.**

It is completely normal that there are things you do not understand when you read. If you do not understand a word or a sentence, it does *not* mean you are "stupid" or "not good enough". It simply means you are in the process of learning English... just like everybody else.

So, what should you do when you find a difficult word? Here are a few ideas:

1. Look at the word and see if it is familiar in any way. Depending on your mother tongue, there might be a similar word in your language. Take a guess - you might surprise yourself!

2. Read the whole sentence many times. As you read that sentence repeatedly, think about everything that has happened in the story. Try to guess the meaning of the whole sentence – not just the difficult word. This takes practice, but is often easier than you think!

3. Make a note of the word in a notebook and check the meaning later.

4. Sometimes, you might find a verb that you do not recognise. Or perhaps you do not understand *why* the verb is being used, and that may frustrate you. But, is it absolutely necessary for you to know this right now? Can you still understand the story? Usually, if you have managed to recognise the main verb, that is enough. Instead of getting frustrated, simply notice how the verb is being used, and then carry on reading!

5. If all the other steps fail, or you simply "have to know" the meaning of a particular word, you can look it up in a dictionary. However, try not to do this unless you have to.

These steps are designed to do something very important: to train you to handle reading independently and without help. The more you can develop this skill, the better you will be at reading. And, of course, the more you can read, the more you will learn!

Remember that the purpose of reading is *not* to understand every word in the story. The purpose of reading is simply to enjoy the story! Therefore, if you do not understand a word and you cannot guess what the word means from the context, simply try to keep reading. Learning to be happy without understanding everything you read in English is a powerful skill to have because you become an independent and intelligent learner.

The Six-Step Reading Process

1. Read the first chapter of the story all the way through. Your aim is simply to reach the end of the chapter. Do not stop to look up words in the dictionary and do not worry if there are things you do not understand. Simply try to follow the story.

2. When you reach the end of the chapter, read the summary of the plot to see if you have understood what has happened. If you find this too difficult, do not worry.

3. Go back and read the same chapter again. If you like, you can read in more detail than before. Otherwise, simply read it one more time and enjoy!

4. At the end of the chapter, read the summary again, and then try to answer the comprehension questions to check your understanding of what happened. If you do not get them all correct, do not worry.

5. By this point, you should start to understand the main events of the chapter. If you wish, continue to re-read the chapter using the dictionary to check difficult words. You may need to do this a few times until you feel confident. This is normal, and each time you read you will gradually understand more.

6. Otherwise, you should move on to the next chapter and enjoy the rest of the story at your own pace, just like any other book.

Remember, at every stage of the process, there will be words and phrases you do not understand. Instead of worrying, try to focus instead on everything that you *have* understood. Congratulate yourself for taking the time to read in English.

Most of the benefit you get from this book will come from reading each story from beginning to end. Only once you have reached the end of the story should you go back study the language from the story in more depth.

Annexes to each chapter

- Summary
- Multiple-choice questions
- Answers

STORIES

1. Persistence Pays

Chapter 1

"Why can't we come in?," I asked the large man standing in front of us. He was wearing a dark suit, and he was tall and strong. He was blocking the door to Zara's Nightclub. We could hear the loud dance music behind the door. We wanted to go in!

I had lost my job the other day. I needed to have a night of fun! I didn't want to have a lot of stress, so we had to find a way to get inside!

The tall man was a bouncer; his job was to let the "right" people in, and to keep everyone else out. He pointed to his clipboard and frowned. "Your name isn't on this list."

I looked up at him. He was at least six inches taller than me.

"How do we get on that list?"

My friends--Nate and Aaron--and I had dressed up. We had driven across town to come to Zara's. The new club was famous and we wanted to check it out.

But, the bouncer did not reply. Instead, he looked over my skinny shoulder. There was a long line of people behind me.

"How do I get in?" I asked again and I snapped my fingers. I was trying to get his attention.

"You don't," he said. He waved the next guest in the line to come forward. She was a beautiful blonde girl. When I saw her, I had an idea...

"Wait, wait!" I protested. "Our girlfriends are already inside!" It was a lie. Aaron looked at me in a strange way. Perhaps he thought, "Is Jack crazy?"

"Jack, what are you doing?" Aaron yelled in my ear. He was a good-looking guy, but he was also shy. He never took any risks.

"Be quiet," I whispered back. I didn't want the bouncer to hear.

But, he did hear us. He rolled his eyes and tried to ignore me again.

"No, really," I persisted. "Our girlfriends are inside, waiting for us."

He lifted a red velvet rope to let the blonde girl pass.

"Thanks Bruce," she said as she walked by him. I could smell her perfume. I wanted to follow her in, but Bruce, the bouncer, shook his head at me.

"Are your friends really inside?"

"Yes," I answered. "Our girlfriends!"

His expression was doubtful. He rubbed his bald head, then he lifted his clipboard again. "Okay. What are their names?"

"Their...names?" Well, I didn't know their names...because they didn't exist! "Uhh..."

"You're done," he said. He smiled and he pushed me aside. "Next!"

*

We could not get in, so we left Zara's. We went across the street for coffee.

"That was dumb, Jack," Aaron said, and he took off his jacket. He had put on his favourite clothes to come out. With his good looks and clothes, he could be an actor, but his attitude was always negative.

I felt bad because it had been my idea to go out. Everyone knew it was impossible to get inside Zara's without a reservation...and reservations were impossible to get! But, I had wanted to try.

Nate ordered his coffee black, along with two chocolate-glazed donuts. Nate was very different from Aaron. He was more adventurous and happy. Nate loved to eat sweets like cakes and candies, so he was a bit overweight.

"I'll have the same," Aaron told the waiter. "But, unglazed donuts please."

"And what would you like, sir?" the waiter asked me.

"I would like to know how to get into that nightclub," I told him.

"You can't get in there. Not without a reservation...or a date," he said. "Unless you are a female, of course. It is easy for the girls to go in. They want more girls inside."

"Why?" Aaron asked.

"Because the guys will go there and spend money!"

I nodded. "That's unfair."

The waiter shrugged his shoulders. "Maybe, but that's life. If you want to go to Zara's, you will have to find someone to go with you. You want to order anything?"

"Just coffee with milk. No donuts." I looked at my friends. "Who eats donuts at nine o'clock at night?"

Nate and Aaron exchanged looks. "We do," they said together. I sighed and crossed my arms. It looked like I was going to be spending the evening with these two.
*

After our coffees (and donuts) were finished, we paid our check. I noticed three girls sitting at a table. They were talking. They were also finished with their food and drinks.

"Guys, look," I said to my friends. "What if--"

"No," Aaron said, cutting off my sentence. "Jack, let's just go."

"Wait. What, Jack?" Nate asked. "Do you want to talk to them?"

I combed my black hair back with my fingers. "We can try. Why not? Come on, I just lost my job. Do me a favour! What is the worst thing that can happen?"

Aaron stared at me, but Nate punched him in the arm. "Come on, Aaron!" he said. "Jack is right. We can ask them. Perhaps they will want to go with us to Zara's. If we get inside, they can stay with us. Or, they can leave us if they want to."

The girls were watching us. One of them, a girl with red hair, leaned over the table. She whispered something to her friends and they nodded. None of them were smiling.

I felt a lump in my throat, but decided to go forward. I walked over to their table. My friends stayed behind me.

"Hi, my name is Jack Cruz. No relationship to Tom Cruise," I said, making a bad joke.

"Clearly," the redhead said. Her friends laughed, but I laughed with them. A little.

"Would you like to go to Zara's with us? The bouncer would not let us in," I said. "But maybe, we could get in with dates."

The smallest of the three girls said, "Dates? We don't even know you!"

"I know," I said. "But let's just try! Don't you want to see inside Zara's?"

The girls looked through the window at the long line in front of the nightclub. Then they looked at each other.

"We don't need you to get inside," said the redhead. "But...I guess we can help you boys out. By the way, my name is Caprice."

Annex to Chapter 1

Summary

Jack Cruz has lost his job. He and his friends, Nate and Aaron, go out to a nightclub named Zara's, but they cannot get in. They do not have reservations. They go across the street to have coffee and donuts in a café. They see a group of girls in the cafe. They ask the girls if they would like to go to the club together. The girls agree.

Multiple-choice questions
Select one answer for each question

1. What is the bouncer's job at Zara's?
   a. He serves drinks
   b. He parks cars
   c. He decides who gets inside
   d. He runs the cash register

2. What gives Jack an idea about how to get inside?
   a. Seeing a blonde girl go inside
   b. Seeing a blonde man go inside
   c. Seeing a couple go inside
   d. Having coffee and donuts

3. Why does Jack think Nate is a little overweight?
   a. Nate doesn't exercise
   b. Nate likes sweet foods like glazed donuts
   c. Nate is shy
   d. None of the above

4. Jack makes a joke about not being related to an actor, but he thinks the joke is:

a. a little funny
b. very funny
c. not very funny at all
d. too serious

5. The girls:
    a. are excited to date the boys
    b. are angry for being bothered
    c. say they will help
    d. will not help

Answers to Chapter 1

1. c
2. a
3. b
4. c
5. c

Chapter 2

"Let me talk to the bouncer," I said, as the six of us left the café.

"No," Caprice said, "Let me. You couldn't talk your way in before."

I began to protest, but Nate nudged me in the ribs. "She's right. Give her a chance."

We started walking toward the back of the line. Caprice grabbed my hand suddenly. We ran toward the bouncer. The others followed us. They did not understand her plan.

"Excuse me, Bruce?" she shouted, waving her hand in the air. She stopped only inches away from the intimidating bouncer. "You're Bruce, aren't you?"

"Do I know you?"

"You were supposed to let my boyfriend in earlier," she said, pointing at me. "What happened?"

"His name wasn't on the list..."

"The list? Do you mean the fake list?" she asked, grabbing at his precious clipboard. He pulled it away from her and held it up, but she was persistent. "Get real! It's a bunch of fake names on a piece of paper."

"How do you know?" Bald Bruce asked, as he bent down to get closer to her. Perhaps he did not want the rest of the line to hear. "And, so what if it is fake?"

"Do you know a woman named Zara Bernhart?"

Bruce stiffened. "The owner?"

"Yeah, the owner." Caprice reached into her handbag. She took out a photograph and her driver's license. She showed both to the bouncer and his face turned pale. "I'm Caprice Bernhart. Zara's my mom."

*

"That was awesome," I said, brushing my black hair out of my eyes. "I had no idea who you were!"

"Were?" Caprice said, leading me to the bar. "I still am! What are you having?"

Several customers were trying to get the helpless bartender's attention, but when he saw Caprice, he walked over to her. "Nice to see you!" he shouted over the music. "Can I get you something?"

"A Coke," she said, "and..." She looked at me.

"Me, too."

"What?" the bartender asked. "Sorry, I couldn't hear you, man!"

"I'll have a Coke too!" I yelled.

Caprice seemed surprised by my order. "Don't you drink alcohol?"

"I'm underage," I said, smiling.

"I hope not," she said, "or we're both in trouble." The bartender brought over our sodas. We took them to a table in a vacant corner. "Your friends disappeared."

"I see one of them on the dance floor," I said, pointing to Nate. He was dancing with the smallest of the girls. "They seem to get along! Look, they are smiling."

"What about the other one?"

"Aaron? He's...gone!" I could not see Aaron anywhere. I took my phone out of my pocket because I wanted to check my messages. Perhaps he had sent me a text message. Yes, he had texted me! "Looks like he decided to go home."

"Hey, guys," said the third girl, as she walked over to our table. "What's up?"

"Where were you?" Caprice asked. "Did you scare Aaron away?"

"I guess so," she said. Then she looked at me. "By the way, what's your name again?"

"Jack," I said. "And I'm sorry, you are...?"

"I'm Susan. The other girl's Aisha. Anyways, your friend was weird!"

"He's not weird, he's shy," I said. "As The Smith's song goes, 'shyness is nice, and shyness can stop you...'"

"'...from doing all the things in life you'd like to!'" Susan finished. "I love that song!"

"Really? They are one of my favourite bands--"

"Hey, you scared away your boyfriend," Caprice said to her friend. "Leave my date alone!"

Susan smirked. She was unhappy. "Fine. I'm going to the bar," she said, "and I'm putting my drinks on your tab. You will have to pay for them later!" She walked away. She went to stand in the crowd in front of the busy bar.

I was happy to hear myself called a "date."

"Thanks again for helping us," I said. "It was a hard week for me. It was difficult because I lost my job this week."

"Oh, that's terrible! What was your job?" She looked uncomfortable.

Why did I tell her I'd lost my job? I thought.

"Actually," I said, pointing at the bar. "I did that. I was a bartender."

She bit her lip. She was thinking of something. "So," she said at last, "Is Zara's everything you dreamed of?"

I looked around the club. It had an expensive disco lighting system. It also had very loud audio speakers on the walls. A professional DJ was playing the best music, and the dance floor was packed. But, there were also plenty of seats for people to sit and talk.

"I love it," I said. "I would love to come here every week."

"Is that a hint?"

"Yes," I said. "I mean, if you want to act like you are my date again. I would love to call you...if you give me your phone number."

Caprice grinned and put out her hand. I reached out to take it, but she stopped me. "No, give me your phone."

"Oh." I handed over my phone. She took it and added herself to my contacts list.

"So now you have it. Don't post it on the Internet. It's private."

Immediately, I dialled her number. I watched her phone light up. "Now you have my number too," I said. "You can put mine on the Internet. I don't mind. Nobody ever tries to call me."

"Your mother doesn't own a nightclub," she said. "Does she?"

"I don't think so," I said, laughing. "Listen, I really want you to know...I did not know who you were when I talked to you in the café."

"I believe you," she said. "I know you weren't just trying to use me."

"Well, I was trying to use you," I admitted, "but I was very honest about it."

This time, she laughed and looked away. *Maybe I need to shut up*, I thought.

"I need to get going soon," she said. "I told my roommate I would be home before eleven."

"You should live for yourself, not for others," I said. "I read that on a card or something."

Caprice gave me a wide grin. "I agree one hundred percent! But, my roommate lost her keys to the apartment. Do you think she should wait outside while I stay here with you?"

26

I made an innocent face. "I don't mind if she waits."

"Typical male," she said, standing up. "You have my number."

"You have mine," I said, getting up with her. I wanted to walk her to the exit. "Let's see who calls the other first. We could place a bet."

For a moment, her face turned serious. "Never bet against me or my family, Jack. We have a history of never losing."

Annex to Chapter 2

Summary

Jack and his friends are able to get into Zara's nightclub with the help of Caprice and her friends. Jack and Caprice order drinks at the bar. Jack learns a secret--that Caprice's family owns the club. Nate dances with Aisha, but Aaron leaves. Caprice gives Jack her phone number and prepares to leave too.

Multiple-choice questions
Select one answer for each question

6. Caprice is able to convince the bouncer to let them inside by:
   a. giving him money
   b. punching his arm
   c. showing him proof that her family owns the club
   d. lying

7. Jack goes to the bar with Caprice. He:
   a. does not order a drink
   b. orders the same drink as her
   c. orders a beer
   d. orders a Coke and nachos

8. Aaron sends Jack a message on his phone. Aaron:
   a. left with the girl he met
   b. is on the dance floor with the girl he met
   c. left by himself
   d. wants to come sit with Jack and Caprice

9. Caprice gives Jack her phone number by:

a. writing it on a napkin
b. whispering in his ear
c. calling him
d. putting it into his phone herself

10. Jack and Caprice almost make a bet, but they do not bet because:
    a. Caprice is religious and does not bet
    b. Jack cannot hear her
    c. Aaron sends Jack a message not to bet her
    d. Caprice knows Jack would lose the bet

6. c
7. b
8. c
9. d
10. d

Chapter 3

I waited three days before calling her. It was a long three days. It was hard to wait.

"You lose," Caprice said when she answered the phone.

"We didn't bet, remember? I was wondering...what are you doing tonight?"

She paused. She did not say anything for a moment. "My parents are having a small party at home. Some business partners are coming to their house. They want to talk about the nightclub. They are curious how it is doing."

"Are you going to go?" I asked.

"Yes, because they want my opinion. They want the opinion of a younger person. Maybe you should come over too!"

I laughed about that. "No! You want me to meet your parents? And you want me to talk about my opinion of their club?"

Caprice didn't laugh with me. "Yes. I want you to come. Why not? I think you are a very honest person--"

"But, you do not know me!"

"Women have intuition about people, Jack. Can you meet me by eight?"

*

We met outside her apartment. We took her car to her parents' home. The home was a giant mansion. There were two stories and twenty rooms. I counted the windows.

"What are you doing?" she asked me. She drove her car up the large driveway.

"I'm counting the windows."

"Why?"

"I don't know. I am trying to see where the restroom is."

That was a dumb thing to say, I decided. I'd never been to a rich person's house before. Now I was going to have dinner with rich strangers. The strangers were this girl's parents!

I had good reasons to be nervous.

"Don't be nervous," she said. She was getting out of the car. "Just be yourself."

"What does that mean? People always say that! 'Be yourself, be yourself.' Of course I will be myself!"

"Okay, never mind," she said. She closed the car door hard. "You are acting weird. Be somebody else."

"Sorry. This night is weird. I don't know what to say to your parents."

She knocked on the door. A butler answered. A butler!

"Hi, Jeeves," she said.

You're butler is not named Jeeves! I wanted to say.

"Very funny, young lady. Come inside. And welcome, mister...?"

"Hi, I'm Jack Cruz," I said. I held out my hand.

The butler shook my hand. He said his real name was Pete, not Jeeves. He took us to the large living room. There were a dozen people sitting on sofas. Two of them stood up. They walked over to Caprice and me.

"Hi darling," said a beautiful lady. She looked like Caprice, but she was older. "Is this your new friend? Hi, I'm Zara."

"I'm Jack," I said, and I held out my hand again. She did not shake my hand. Instead, she gave me a big hug. A handsome man with grey hair was standing behind her.

"My wife likes hugs," he said. "But I'll shake your hand." His handshake was like Superman's. "Call me Ismael."

I remembered the joke about the butler's name. I thought he was making a joke too. "Ismael? You are funny! You cannot fool me again," I said.

"No, it isn't a joke," Caprice said. "My dad's name is Ismael."

Zara laughed out loud. "I like your friend, Caprice," she said. "Please sit down, Jack. Let's chat."

*

We talked for a few minutes in the living room. Then, we moved to the dining room. Dinner was a delicious chicken curry. After dinner, we started to talk about their nightclub business.

"What was your impression of the place?" Zara asked.

"My impression? Well, the first thing I saw was the bouncer. He was not rude, but I do not think his reservation list is real."

"You think the reservation list is fake? Why do you think that?"

Caprice and I smiled at each other. "I told him it wasn't real," Caprice said.

"Many people want to come to the club," Zara said. She was moving her pearl necklace around her shirt collar. "We have to be careful. We cannot let everyone inside. There isn't enough room for everyone."

"There is another reason," Caprice's father said. "Some people want to come, but not spend money. Other people come to spend money. It's a business. We want customers with money."

"What do you think about the inside?" Zara asked. "Did you like it?"

I remembered the poor bartender. He was trying to help too many customers. I had been a bartender too. I knew it was a hard job.

"I liked the inside, but you need an extra bartender," I said. "Your guy needed help. He had too many customers. There was a very big crowd. I felt sorry for him."

"Do you know any bartenders? Do you know anyone who needs a job?" Caprice asked. Zara and Ismael waited for my answer.

"Hmmm, yes. I do know a bartender that needs a job," I said. "And he works cheap."

*

By the end of the week, I had a new job--at Zara's Nightclub! My girlfriend, Caprice, came to visit me often. I became friends with the other bartender, Dennis. I also became friends with Bruce, the bouncer.

"I can't believe it. You are lucky, Jack," Aaron said one night. He was shaking his head.

"Lucky?" I asked. Aaron was sitting alone. He sat beside Nate and Nate's new girlfriend, Aisha. "You're wrong, my friend. Luck was not the reason. Luck had nothing to do with it. It was persistence. In this life, persistence is the only way to get anything."

"Luckily," Caprice said, holding my hand, "Jack has plenty of that!"

Annex to Chapter 3

Summary

Jack calls Caprice. She invites Jack to meet her parents and give his opinion of the club. Jack is very impressed by their fancy home. He meets their butler, then Zara and Ismael, Caprice's parents. They have dinner. He tells them his opinions, then he ends up getting a new job a Zara's as a bartender!

Multiple-choice questions
Select one answer for each question

11. Caprice invites Jack to:
    a. her apartment
    b. Zara's Nightclub
    c. her parents' home
    d. a job interview

12. Jack is nervous about:
    a. meeting Caprice's parents
    b. going on another date with Caprice
    c. his bad breath
    d. the fact that he does not have a job

13. Caprice introduces her parents' butler as "Jeeves."
    a. She was joking
    b. The butler's name really is Jeeves
    c. The butler's name is Bruce
    d. None of the above

14. When Zara meets Jack, she:
    a. shakes his hand

b. introduces her husband
c. laughs at him
d. gives him a hug

15. The first thing Jack says about the nightclub is:
    a. he would change the name of it
    b. he would hire another bartender
    c. he doesn't like the reservation list
    d. he wants a job there

11. c
12. a
13. a
14. d
15. c

2. A List of Lies

Chapter 1

World War II Germany...

"Surrender now!" a German voice shouted. He was outside. His jeep's engine was loud, but he was louder. "Come out or we will open fire!"

Lily did not look out of the broken window. She was inside an old building. It was surrounded by Nazi soldiers. If she did not surrender, they would shoot. They would keep shooting until the building fell down!

"Okay!" she yelled. She was hiding in the corner of a dark room. Her brown bag was next to her. Inside the bag was a secret, and her job was to keep it safe. "I am coming out! I will come out from the front door!"

She waited and listened.

"Put your hands up! Put them in the air or we will shoot you," the soldier said. "If you are holding anything, we will shoot you!"

They really want to shoot me, Lily thought, checking her gun. *I want to shoot a few of them too. They killed my partner...*

There was no time to think about the past. Lily did not have time for emotions now.

She was a professional. She had a job to do.

Surrendering was not a part of her plan.

She tied her red hair in a ponytail. Crawling on her hands and knees, she moved across the room. She moved down the hallway. She went toward the back door.

"Come out! You have five seconds!"

If I come out, you will kill me, she thought. Suddenly, she turned left, away from the back door. There was a small wooden door in front of her. It went to a basement.

She opened it and ran down the stairs. *They know about this basement, but they don't know it goes to a tunnel!*

Above her, she heard the sound of powerful gunfire...machine guns shooting the building. They would tear the building apart.

Lily knew the soldiers were told not to kill her, but they *were* trying to kill her. They knew she was dangerous.

Someone told them who I am. I had a secret identity, but that is gone now.

Now every Nazi in Germany wants me dead...except the ones in charge. The bosses want me alive. They want to ask me questions...

The basement smelled bad. It was not very bright; it only had one old light bulb. In front of her was an old carpet. The carpet hung from the ceiling. Lily pulled it down. Behind the carpet was a large hole.

The tunnel!

She was going to escape through the tunnel...but what was on the other side? She did not know. Perhaps someone was waiting for her?

The gunfire stopped. The sound of the jeep engine also stopped. The leader of the soldiers was shouting. He was speaking German. Lily knew German, and she understood what he was saying.

"Go inside! Don't come out until you find her! Look in the basement too!"

I have to go, Lily decided. She took out the light bulb. The basement and the tunnel were completely black. She didn't care. Lily Z. Bernhart was America's greatest female spy. She had finished thirty-eight missions. She always succeeded in her missions.

And, she was not afraid of the dark.

*

Three hours later...

Lily sat in a cafe in Berlin. She was smoking a cigarette. She watched a thin waiter walk by her. He was ignoring her. Why was he ignoring her? She had red hair and her face looked like a foreigner's face.

Maybe he did not like foreigners.

"Excuse me!" she said in German. "Do you see me?"

On most days, Lily did not bring attention to herself. She was a professional spy. Lily did not walk around in fancy clothes. She did not drive fast cars.

She was very healthy, but she did not look like a model.

Sometimes, people asked her name. She never said, "Bernhart. Lily Bernhart."

The government had given her a dozen fake names. There was no reason to use her real name.

Normally, she acted shy. But, she wanted service. She was thirsty and needed a drink.

"Excuse me!" she repeated.

"Yes? Can I help you?" the waiter asked. There were not many customers. The café was not busy.

"Bring me a coffee and an apple pastry."

He turned and went behind the counter. He poured the coffee. He put the pastry on a plate. Then, she watched him walk to the kitchen.

Why is he going to the kitchen? Everything I want is there, at the counter!

She knew why he had left. He went to use a telephone. He was going to call the soldiers. He was going to say--*the lady with red hair is here!*

Lily stopped her thoughts. *I'm being silly,* she said to herself.

Then, she saw him. He was looking at her from the kitchen window.

His nose looks broken, she thought.

The thin waiter brought her coffee and a pastry. He put them on the table.

She noticed he was sweating.

The weather was cold. Why was he sweating? Was he nervous? He wiped the sweat with his shirt sleeve.

"Anything else?"

"No," she said, drinking her coffee. The coffee was cold.

"Are you a tourist? Your German is very good," he said. He tried to smile, but his smile did not look real.

She shook her head and she looked at his broken nose.

"I live here. I've lived here many years."

He was looking at her bag. *Something is not right,* she thought. *First, he ignored me. Now, he is paying too much attention to me.*

"Please let me know if you need anything else, Miss...?"

"Bolan. Nellie Bolan."

The waiter left.

I am getting paranoid, she thought. She lit a cigarette.

Smoking was a bad habit, but her job was dangerous. There were many things to worry about. Smoking was bad, but some things were worse like other spies, and Nazi soldiers, and people who helped the Nazis...

Lily was almost done eating her pastry. She heard a familiar sound – the sound of a jeep engine.

The soldiers were here!

She stood up fast. The waiter was in front of the kitchen door. Lily took her brown bag and her fork. She pushed the table away. She ran toward the waiter. She was holding the fork in front of her.

The thin waiter jumped out of her way. Lily ran through the kitchen. She escaped from the back door of the café.

She ran into the night, but she knew the soldiers would follow her.

Annex to Chapter 1

Summary

Lily is hiding in a house. She is hiding from German soldiers. The soldiers are Nazis. She escapes from the house by using a tunnel. Later, she goes to a café. The waiter ignores her, but then he gives her a lot of attention. Too much attention. Lily thinks he called the soldiers. She is right! The Nazis arrive and she escapes again.

Multiple-choice questions
Select one answer for each question

1. When Lily is hiding in the house, what does she have?
    a. A bag and a phone
    b. A coat and a gun
    c. A bag and a gun
    d. A pastry and a coffee

2. How does she escape the house?
    a. She surrenders
    b. She uses the back door
    c. She uses a tunnel
    d. A waiter helps her

3. Lily is a spy. She likes:
    a. fast cars
    b. fancy clothes
    c. German music
    d. smoking cigarettes

4. At the restaurant, the waiter goes to the kitchen to:
    a. get the coffee

b. make a phone call
c. make the pastry
d. wash his hands

5. Lily hears something outside. It scares her. What does she hear?
    a. A jeep engine
    b. A soldier shouting
    c. Guns shooting
    d. Someone calling her name

Answers to Chapter 1

1. c
2. c
3. d
4. b
5. a

Chapter 2

"Why did you come here?" the small old man asked. He was not happy; he did not like late night visitors. And, he did not like Nazis. "Are you being followed?"

Lily held up her brown bag. "I need a place to hide."

"Are the Nazis following you?" he asked again.

"No," she lied.

He pointed to the bag. "What is in the bag?"

"Let me in and I will tell you."

"No." The small man closed the door. Lily knocked again, quietly. She did not want neighbours to hear.

"Go away!" the man said. He was behind the door. "Go! Take your secrets away!"

Lily looked behind her. The soldiers were out there. They were looking for her. She needed to hide--fast! She had to get off the street.

"David! David, if you do not let me in, they will catch me," she said. She pushed her face against the door. "If they catch me, they will ask questions. They will ask who helped me."

"I am not helping you!"

"But, I will tell them you did."

She did not like to scare people, but her mission was important. She could not let the Nazis catch her. She could not let them get her bag...

The door opened. The small man was holding a gun. "I could kill you," he said. "Get inside. Now!"

*

"I need to use your restroom," she said.

"Too bad." David pointed the gun at her head. "Give me the bag."

"I came here to hide. I did not come here to give away my secrets."

"If I shoot you, I will take the bag," he said.

"You will not shoot. You will help me. I need to go to the American Embassy."

"Sit down."

Lily sat down at the small wood table. He sat by her. He smelled very bad. Perhaps he did not have water in his home.

He was still holding the gun. Outside, they heard a jeep. No, many jeeps!

"They are coming..." she said. "You have to trust me."

"Why should I? You will tell them I helped you!"

She took out her cigarettes. She offered one to him. He reached for it.

Lily grabbed his gun. She was fast.

She grabbed his wrist with her other hand. He dropped the gun on the table.

"I'll take this," she said, picking up his gun. She looked at it. It was very old. "Does this gun work?"

"No," he said.

She opened her bag and dropped his gun inside. David did not move. He sat and watched her. "I could run outside," he said. "I could say you broke into my home."

"You could try," Lily said. She took out her gun. "But, you would fail. My gun works fine."

"If you shoot, the soldiers would hear--"

"Enough!" she yelled. She hit the table with her hand. "You will help me. Now! Where is your telephone?"

"I do not have a phone."

Lily stood up. She did not believe him. She looked around the small one-bedroom home. "You are lying."

"Am I? Do you see a phone?"

She went into the bedroom. There was a phone by the bed. "Yes, I see one. Get up! I will tell you the number to call."

*

A few minutes later, Lily hung up the phone.

"My friends are coming. Someone will be here soon. I will leave you alone."

"Are you crazy?" David asked. His eyes were big. He was scared. "Why did you give them my address? The soldiers will see the foreigners coming to my house. You put my life in danger."

"David, this is a war. We are all in danger."

"But, I am not a fighter!" he said. "I am an old man!"

She brushed her red hair off her face. She was tired. "David, do you remember when we met?"

He nodded. "You helped my niece. A soldier was bothering her."

"I was almost arrested, but I helped her," Lily said. She put her gun away. "I brought her here. Remember? I brought her to your home. She was safe."

"Yes. The police came here too. They followed you to my home."

"What did they do?" She walked to the living room, and David followed her.

"They asked questions. They asked me about you."

"What did you say?"

"I said I did not know you. That was the truth," he said.

"And, what did they say?"

He paused. There were tears in his eyes. He was very scared and sad. "They said you are a spy. They wanted me to call them...if you returned."

48

Lily looked at him closely. He saw she had beautiful green eyes.

"Will you call them?" she asked. She looked sad too.

"Help an American spy...or help the Nazis," he said. "I don't want to help any of you! Please leave me alone!"

Lily heard a motorcycle outside.

That must be my ride, she thought. *Good. I am ready to leave.*

She opened the door and looked out. The motorcycle driver waved to her.

"My ride is here," she said. Lily put her gun inside the bag. She kept his broken gun too.

She took out some money and threw it on the floor. "I am like you, David. I do not want to live in a world of spies and Nazis. If we beat the Nazis, perhaps we will not need spies."

Lily ran outside. She got on the motorcycle. They drove away quickly.

She looked over her shoulder. She knew she had not said the truth.

The world would always have spies...

Annex to Chapter 2

Summary

Lily goes to an old man's house. His name is David.
She wants to hide, but he does not want to help her. He is
afraid. He thinks the Nazis will see her. David points a gun
at her, but she takes it away. Lily uses his telephone to call
for help. She tells him to remember that she helped his niece
once in the past. Her ride comes and she leaves.

Multiple-choice questions
Select one answer for each question

6. David is afraid to help Lily because:
    a. the Nazis know she is there
    b. the Nazis may have seen her go there
    c. he thinks she is a Nazi
    d. he is afraid she will rob him

7. Lily says she needs to use the restroom, and David:
    a. does not let her
    b. shows her where to go
    c. says he does not have water in his home
    d. asks her to wait

8. Lily offers David a cigarette because:
    a. she wants to be friends
    b. he does not have any money to buy cigarettes
    c. she does not want to smoke by herself
    d. none of the above

9. Lily and David know each other because:
    a. they went to school together

b. Lily helped David's niece
c. David helped Lily's niece
d. David is helping the American government

10. After Lily makes her phone call, why is David mad?
    a. Because the call was expensive
    b. Because she gave his name and birthdate
    c. Because she said he was helping her
    d. Because she gave his address

6. b
7. a
8. d
9. b
10. d

Chapter 3

"You failed your mission," the agent said. He did not tell Lily his name.

They were sitting in a small office. The office was inside an empty warehouse.

The agent with no name was wearing a large blue coat and a white shirt. He fixed his red necktie. He was sick and he coughed a lot. "Perhaps we should give you to the Germans."

"I did my job. I got what I was told to get," Lily argued. "I got the folder."

She pointed at the folder. The folder had been in her bag. Now it was on the desk in front of her. She was going to speak again, but the agent raised his hand. He stopped her from talking.

"Yes," he said, frowning. "You got it. Good job."

"So, why are you angry?"

"Because," he said, "inside the folder was information. Very important information."

"Was the information there?"

"Half of it was. Only half."

Lily's face turned pale. "What? You are saying half is missing?"

"That's right. Where is the other half?"

She shrugged her shoulders. "I don't know. I robbed the office you told me to. I took the folder..."

"Did you open this folder?"

"Of course not," she said. "That is not my job."

"But, you know what is inside of it?"

Lily shook off her shoes. They were uncomfortable and her feet hurt. She took out a cigarette.

The agent with no name took the cigarette away.

"I asked you a question, Miss Livesay--"

"Are you an idiot? Yes, I know what is inside the folder!" She took out another cigarette and lit it. "I was told to find that folder. There it is. And inside--"

"Inside is a list of names. Americans who are working for the Nazis."

"Then my job is done," Lily said.

"Our man told us the list was bigger. He said there were three hundred names." The agent in the blue coat opened the folder. He took out some papers. "I counted. There are only one hundred and forty-nine names."

He's lying, she thought. *There were one hundred and fifty names on the list.*

"What do you want?" she asked. "I was chased by Nazis! I was almost shot for that list!"

The agent coughed. He walked backward. He did not like the smoke. "You have a dangerous job. You have been successful...in the past. But, I will report this failure. I must tell your boss. He can decide what to do."

My boss is a woman, Lily thought. *He's lying again!*

She looked around the office. "Where is my boss?"

"He will come here later. You must wait here."

"You said my mission is not finished. Half of the list is missing," she said. "I will go out again."

"No. You cannot leave. They know who you are," he said, opening a window. He put his head outside for a moment.

"Are you looking for something?" she asked.

He closed the window. "I wanted some fresh air."

He waited for her to finish smoking. "They know who you are," he repeated. "So you cannot go back out."

"I have a question for you," she said. "The list of names. Those are American government workers?"

54

The agent with no name sneezed. He took out a tissue. He wiped his nose. "Yes."

"Those people are working for the Nazis?"

"Correct." He put the papers back in the folder.

"We will find the people on the list." She leaned forward on the desk. She touched the folder, but he took it away.

"Yes, we will find them all."

"What will happen to them?"

"You know what will happen," he said. "They will be investigated. If they are really spying for the Germans, we will learn. We know what to do with people who turn against America."

"Kill them?" Lily asked. Slowly, she moved her bag. She moved it closer to her.

"Yes. If they are Americans working for the Nazis...they must die."

I agree, she decided. Lily had not told the agent everything.

She had opened the folder.

She knew where the other information was...because she had it. She had the other half of the list.

But, Lily was always paranoid. She never trusted anyone. That is why she had not told him yet.

When the agent looked away, Lily took a gun out of her bag. He turned to her. She pointed the gun at his stomach.

"What do you think you are doing?" he asked.

"Do you know how to count?" she asked him. "Can you count to one hundred and fifty?"

He closed his eyes. "You are making a big mistake," he said.

"You saw your own name on the list. Didn't you?"

"Miss Livesay, put that gun down. I work for your boss."

"What's his name?" Lily asked.

"It does not matter," he said. "You don't know his real name anyway."

"My boss is a woman," she said, smiling. "And, you don't know my real name either."

The agent opened his eyes. Lily thought he looked afraid, but she was not sure...

"Here," she said. She put the gun on the desk. "I trust you. You can have my gun."

He looked at her face, then at the gun. Quickly, he reached out. He picked up the gun from the table. Outside, they could hear jeeps coming...

"Where did you get this old gun?" he asked, laughing. Then, he pointed it at her. "I thought you would use a better gun. Well, it does not matter. You were right. Yes, my name was on the list, but you will never tell anyone."

He pulled the trigger, but the gun did not fire.

She took out her own gun. "You are right too," she said. "I do use a better gun."

Lily shot the agent three times. He fell down on the ground. She took the folder and put it back into her bag, then she ran outside. The motorcycle driver was there. He was watching the jeeps.

"Look, the Nazis are coming!" he yelled. "Did you finish your business?"

"Yes," she said. "My mission is over. Let's get out of here!"

Annex to Chapter 3

Summary

Lily meets a government agent. She does not know his name. He is unhappy because she did not finish her mission. She found a folder with names in it, but he says half of the names are missing. The names are people who are spying for the Nazis. Lily learns that the agent is lying to her. He is also working for the Nazis. She shoots him and escapes...again!

Multiple-choice questions
Select one answer for each question

11. The agent with no name is angry because:
    a. Lily did not bring all the names he wanted
    b. Lily hid at David's house
    c. Lily did not like him
    d. Lily took her shoes off

12. The agent with no name was coughing because:
    a. the office was dirty
    b. he was sick
    c. he was allergic to smoke
    d. none of the above

13. The folder had a list of names. The list was:
    a. missing fifty names
    b. missing half of the names
    c. missing only one name
    d. not missing anything

14. Lily put a gun on the table because:
    a. she trusted the agent

b. she knew it was broken
c. she knew she would be faster to shot than the agent
d. she had taken the bullets out of it first

15. Why did Lily shoot the agent?
    a. Because he was about to kill her
    b. It was an accident
    c. Because she was afraid of him
    d. Because he was a spy for the Nazis

11. a
12. b
13. b
14. b
15. d

3. A Terrible Town

Chapter 1

"You two can go on your big adventure," Ari said. "But I am staying home!"

"No, you are not. You are coming with us!" Denza tried to pick her friend up. Ari kicked her in the knee. She put him down.

Ari was eighty years old. He was not a human though. Ari was a Sliwoh with long white hair. His fingers were long and wrinkly.

Ari was very young...for a Sliwoh. Compared to humans, he was a teenager.

"No, I'm staying home," Ari repeated. "I will not change my mind. I do not want go out. I don't want to look for treasure, and I don't want to fight anybody. You can keep your adventure!"

Denza raised her hairy arms in the air. "I give up!" she said. She was also a Sliwoh, but she was very loud and playful. Most Sliwohs were not.

The other friend was a Glowman. Glowmen loved fighting, they loved adventure, and they really loved gold and treasure.

Their favourite thing in the world was treasure.

The Glowman's name was Lummp. No one knew how old Lummp was. Lummp liked to talk a lot, but no one understood him. He did not speak the Sliwoh language, but he could write it.

Lummp carried a notebook. Sometimes, he would write things on paper.

He wrote a note to Ari.

"Ari," the note said, "you can stay home."

"Thank you," Ari said. "See? Lummp agrees with me."

"No, I don't," Lummp wrote. He pointed out the window. Far away was a cloud of dust. There were horses coming. Ari could see humans on the horses. Humans! One of the men was wearing a long yellow coat. He was wearing a crown on his head.

"We do not have to leave for adventure," Denza said with a smile. "Adventure is coming to us!"

*

Ari, Denza, and Lummp ran outside. Everyone in town was outside. Their town was small. It was called Bird's Field. It was very quiet. Most of the people who lived in Bird's Field were Sliwohs, but there were a few Glowmen and a few other types of persons.

All of them were standing in front of their homes. They were looking at the humans on horses.

Visitors were rare. They never saw strangers, and these strangers were dressed very odd.

The horses slowed down. The first horse was a large black mare. Its rider was the tall man in the yellow coat. There was a crown on his head. He looked like a tired king.

He touched his horse's neck and the horse stood still. The rider climbed down. He looked like the leader of the other men.

"Does anyone here know who I am?" he asked in English. The other horse riders stayed on their horses. There were eight in total, including the leader.

"Why don't you just tell us?" asked a small Sliwoh. It was Pidor, the baker. Pidor, like most Sliwohs, remembered the old English language. "We don't like mysteries here, human!"

Denza walked forward. "Are you a king from the East?" she asked.

"Why do you think I'm a king?"

She pointed to his crown.

The tall man in yellow took the crown off his head. "Perhaps I stole this," he said. He had a long red beard and bright blue eyes.

Lummp was impressed with the crown. It was made of gold. It must be heavy...and worth a lot of money.

"If you stole it," said Pidor, "then go give it back. We don't like thieves here."

"What do you like?" the man asked. "Do you like anything?"

"We like to be left alone." Pidor crossed his arms. One of the other riders came closer to him. The leader waved his hand.

"No," the leader said. "Give the old Sliwoh what he wants. Leave him alone." He looked again at Denza. "You are almost correct. I was a king. I am not a king anymore." He dropped the crown on the ground.

Lummp wrote a note. He showed the note to Denza.

The note said, "Ask him if I can have that crown now."

Denza shook her head. She ignored Lummp.

"What happened?" she asked the former king. "And why did you come to Bird's Field?"

The other riders stopped their horses. They all got down. They stood next to their king.

"These men," he said, "are the last of the humans. There was a great war in the East. Everyone was killed. I am not a king anymore...because there is no one left to rule."

"Then why have you come here?" Pidor asked. His wife stood behind him, hiding their daughters.

"Do not fear for your girls," said the leader, scratching his red beard. "My name is Yardum. I am taking these seven men to the sea town of Spring Field, but we are lost."

"My name is Denza. You need a guide," Denza said, stepping forward.

"Yes, as a matter of fact, I do," Yardum said. "I have no money, but I have this gold crown. I will give it to anyone who helps us."

Ari had a question. "Why must you go to Spring Field? What is there for you?"

"There is a rumour that my friends went there. Perhaps we are not the last humans. I need to find out, so we are on a quest!"

Lummp wrote a note to Denza. He wanted to go because he wanted the crown. Denza nodded; she also wished to go on the journey. "We'll help you," she said.

Ari looked alarmed. He could not allow Denza to go with these strangers. He whispered to her in Sliwohish, but she shook her head. "I'm going," she told him. "Come with us!"

Yardum and his men awaited Ari's answer.

"I just want to stay home," Ari said. "But I will go too."

I will go to protect you, Denza, he thought.

One of the riders who had a scar on his forehead bent and picked up the crown. He wiped off the dirt and put it in a saddlebag, then he got back on his horse.

"It is settled then," Yardum said. "You," he pointed to Lummp, "ride with Sadida, the one with the scar. He will keep the crown for now. "You," he pointed to Ari, "ride with fat Ekin back there. And Denza, you can ride with me."

Annex to Chapter 1

Summary

Ari is a young Sliwoh. He does not like adventure, but his friends, Denza and Lummp, do. Denza is also a Sliwoh, Lummp is a Glowman. They see humans coming to their town, so they go out to meet them. The humans came from the East, they are looking for a sea town to search for other humans. Ari, Denza, and Lummp agree to go with them.

Multiple-choice questions
Select one answer for each question

1. Ari is eighty years old, but he is:
    a. considered an old person
    b. considered to be a teenager
    c. considered to be wise
    d. none of the above

2. Denza and Ari are not humans. They are:
    a. Lummps
    b. Glowmen
    c. horses
    d. Sliwohs

3. Lummp cannot speak their language, but he can:
    a. write it
    b. sing it
    c. communicate with them in English
    d. use sign language

4. Humans come on horses. They are lost and looking for:

a. someone to buy their gold
b. other humans
c. a town called Bird's Field
d. Glowmen

5. Yardum says he was once:
    a. a king
    b. a thief
    c. a baker
    d. a Sliwoh

Answers to Chapter 1

1. b
2. d
3. a
4. b
5. a

Chapter 2

After riding all day, they arrived in the town of Hill Side. Hill Side was a town of mountains and jewel miners. It was also a very dangerous town, full of criminals. All of the jewel miners carried weapons to protect themselves from thieves.

The sun had been down for hours. It was getting late and people were looking at them.

"We must be careful here," Ari said. "We should have gone around Hill Side."

"This way is faster," Denza said. "Besides, no one is going to bother eight large humans."

Maybe not, Ari thought. *But everyone will bother two Sliwohs, and Glowmen never fight. Lummp is no help. We must stay with the humans at all times.*

"We are tired," Yardum said. "The horses need rest. So do I."

"What, you want to stay here?" Ari asked. "Let's keep going. We can camp outside of town."

"We have no camping supplies. Do you want to sleep on the ground with no blanket or tent?"

"No, but--"

"Then we will rent rooms for the night," Yardum said, riding toward a small group of cabins. "Tomorrow morning, we will leave early, so you will not be scared for long, little Sliwohs."

Denza laughed, but Ari was not happy. Yardum and his men tied the horses to wooden posts. Yardum walked to the main cabin.

"You said you don't have any money," Ari said.

The tall, bearded man in yellow turned. "What?"

"Back at Bird's Field...you said you have no money."

Yardum stared at the little Sliwoh. "That is true. What is your point?"

"How will you pay for the rooms?"

The humans looked at their leader. Sadida smiled at Lummp who wrote a "?" on his notebook. Ekin put his heavy hand on Ari's shoulder.

"It is a good question, little Sliwoh," Yardum said. "But don't worry, I will sweet talk them. I'm very persuasive when I need to be."

*

Yardum was indeed very persuasive. He got them four large rooms. One for himself, two rooms for his men, and one for Ari, Denza, and Lummp to share.

Denza took the bed. Ari and Lummp put blankets on the floor. At least, the rooms were warm.

"I don't trust him," Ari said. "How did he get rooms with no money?"

Lummp wrote a note. "Maybe he threatened the owner of the cabins..."

"Yes, that is what I think," Ari said. "He told the cabin owner that his men would hurt them!"

"Keep your voice down," Denza said. "You think Yardum is dangerous? Then don't talk so loud or he'll hear you."

"I'm only saying we do not know him. And now, we are spending the night in Hill Side. This was a bad idea."

"I agree," she said. "Bringing you was a bad idea!"

Lummp laughed. Ari rolled over and tried to go to sleep.

*

The three were finally asleep when the door burst open. Dark figures had broken the door and ran into the small room. Ari sat up, but was hit in the head. He fell back

68

down, crashing into Lummp. They heard Denza scream and saw her being picked up.

Someone was kidnapping her!

Holding his bruised head, Ari got up again. The dark figures were not humans; they looked like miners. Miners were shorter and rounder than most humans. Their skin was very pale because they did not get much sunlight. Their eyes were very big to help them see better in the darkness of the mines.

One miner held Denza and ran outside with her. His hand was over her mouth and she was not making any sound.

The other miner waited at the door for a moment. He looked confused. He was holding something. He had taken Denza's blanket.

Suddenly, Ari heard the sound of the humans coming. They would be able to help!

"Miners have taken Denza!" Ari shouted. He saw Sadida and Ekin running toward him. The second miner ran into the darkness and caught up with the first miner, the one who held Denza.

In the dark, it was hard to see which one held her...and which held the blanket!

Ari was chasing them. He pointed in their direction. "Go after them!" he yelled at the two humans. "They have her!"

Miners were very fast runners. They were already far away. One went left, the other went right.

"Which one has the female?" Ekin asked, running next to Ari.

"I cannot tell," Ari said. "Come with me. We'll chase the left one. Sadida, go right!"

Lummp stayed at the cabin. Glowmen were extremely slow walkers, and they never ran, but when Yardum and the other humans came, Lummp wrote them the story of what happened.

"Do not worry," the former king said. "My men will catch those monsters! They will save your friend."

*

Lummp waited with Yardum and the others. After an hour, Ari, Sadida, and Ekin returned. Denza was not with them.

"I caught one of the miners," Sadida said. "But he did not have the female Sliwoh. He only carried a blanket."

"Did he say where the other miner was going?"

"Yes," the scarred human said, rubbing his fists. "I made him talk. The kidnapper is taking Denza West to the sea towns."

"Why?" Yardum asked. "Are they going to Spring Field like us?"

Sadida nodded his head. "They will try to sell her there."

Ari was startled. "What do you mean, sell her? She is a person, not a horse!"

Yardum's blue eyes were very sad. "There is much you do not know about the world," he said. "You have never left Bird's Field, have you?"

"It isn't safe to leave," Ari said.

"Why isn't it safe?"

"Because bad things happen in the other towns…"

The leader looked down at his feet. "But, you don't know what bad things, do you? All you know is the world 'is not safe'. But you don't know why."

"I never wanted to know why," Ari said, crying. Why had he left his town? He knew he was right to stay home! This was all Denza's fault! And now…now she was gone.

"I understand," Yardum said. "But get dressed. We're leaving now. You are going to learn things you did not want to know."

Annex to Chapter 2

Summary

Ari, Denza, and Lummp ride horses with the humans. They go to the mountain town of Hill Side. Hill Side is a dangerous mining town. It is late at night, so they take rooms. They go to bed, but people break into the Sliwohs' room. They take Denza! Ari alerts the humans, and they run after the kidnappers, but the kidnappers escape with Denza as their prisoner.

Multiple-choice questions
Select one answer for each question

6. Ari is eighty years old, but he is:
   a. miners and criminals
   b. a Sliwoh
   c. horses and jewels
   d. rivers and lakes

7. Yardum rents rooms using:
   a. his money
   b. his gold crown
   c. his persuasion
   d. the horses

8. Who does not trust Yardum?
   a. Denza
   b. Lummp
   c. Ekin
   d. Ari

9. What do the kidnappers take?

a. Lummp and his blanket
b. The crown
c. Denza and her blanket
d. Denza and the crown

10. According to Sadida, the kidnapper said:
    a. the miners killed her
    b. the miners will sell her
    c. the miners lost her
    d. the miners married her

6. b
7. c
8. d
9. c
10. b

Chapter 3

It took two days to get to Spring Field. The sea town was beautiful, the sandy beaches were clean and lovely. The blue sea looked warm and full of life. But, there was no time for fun or fishing.

Denza was still missing. She might be here. She might still be the miner's captive...unless he had sold her.

"I have never seen anything like this," Lummp wrote. "When we find Denza, we should move here!"

Ari agreed. Spring Field looked like a perfect town. But, he did not feel comfortable here.

"There is something wrong about this place," he said to his friend. "Do you feel it?"

Lummp shrugged. Glowmen did not feel very much of anything. They were not very sensitive persons.

Yardum led the way. His black horse was in front. It seemed like he knew where he was going.

"Have you been here before?" Ari asked.

"No."

"Where will we begin our search?"

Yardum waved to Sadida. Sadida rode his horse closer to his leader's.

"What is it, my lord?" Sadida asked Yardum.

The tall human in yellow pointed at Ari. "Tell this Sliwoh where we are going."

"We are going to the slave market," the scarred man said. "Your friend Denza will be there."

"How do you know that?" Ari asked.

"He knows," Ekin said, "because he's smart."

Ari was getting scared. He did not like the feeling he had. "And how do you know where the market is? You said you have never been here!"

Suddenly, Ari realized--he had not seen any people in Spring Field. But then, he saw someone, a pale miner. No, a group of miners!

He looked in the window of a building. There were miners inside. Far away, he saw a miner riding a small horse...no, it was a donkey!

"Sorry," Yardum said. "But we have not been honest with you." He pointed to the left. Not very far way, Ari saw a large fenced area. It looked like a big cage for animals. Inside the cage were many Sliwohs and other creatures. They were being held captive.

"This beautiful town has the largest slave market in the West," Yardum said. "We bring many Sliwohs here. You can see them there. And look, there is your friend!"

"Denza!" Ari yelled. Denza was in the cage. She was alive...but a prisoner.

"You work with the miners," Ari said. "You are helping them!"

"Sometimes," Yardum said "we bring them a Sliwoh or two when we are going to Spring Field to buy guns. The miners make very good guns. Don't they, Ekin?"

"The best," Ekin said, pointing a very good gun at Ari.

*

The humans put Ari and Lummp in the cage. Denza ran over to greet them.

"I thought I would never see you again!" she said. "I am sorry, this is my fault!"

"No, don't say that," Ari said, hugging her. He looked around. There were at least one hundred Sliwohs in the prison. "How long have you been here?" he asked one of them.

"Not long," the young Sliwoh said. "They will sell us today."

"Who are they going to sell us to?"

"We don't know. By the way, my name is Ked. My brother, Hakan, is over there." Ked pointed to a small boy Sliwoh. Hakan did not look well. He looked sick.

"We have to escape," Ari said. He seemed to be one of the oldest Sliwohs in the cage. "Lummp, what can we do to get out of here?"

Lummp frowned. He wasn't a fighter. He did not have any ideas. But then, he watched one of the miners walk over to a donkey. The miner did something, but Ari did not see.

Lummp took out his notebook and wrote a note.

"It is getting dark," he wrote. He drew a picture of a donkey and smiled. "We will wait until it is late at night."

Ari and Denza read the note. They did not understand.

Lummp drew a picture of a key. He pointed to his picture of the donkey. Ari looked over at the real donkeys. One of them was wearing a small leather bag.

Do the guards keep the keys to the cage in that bag? Ari wondered.

Then, they looked at Yardum and his men who were talking to some miners. The humans were laughing. The miners were paying money to Yardum. Then Sadida took out the crown. The miners were impressed by the expensive gold crown. They gave money for it too.

"He lied about everything," Denza said. "He stole that crown like he stole me!"

Yardum looked in her direction, as if he had heard her. He smiled. Denza spit on the ground.

*

Later that night, the humans were gone. They had taken their money and left. All the Sliwohs were on the ground sleeping. The miners had gone to their homes, except for a few guards. Most of the guards were drinking and playing a card game. A few of their donkeys were standing around near the cage. The donkeys were not tied down. They were free to walk around.

When everything was quiet, Lummp tapped Ari on the shoulder. Ari tapped Denza and Ked. None of them were really sleeping. They were pretending. Slowly, all of the Sliwohs got up.

Lummp, the Glowman, held out the palm of his hand. His hand was glowing with a small red light. He waved his hand at the donkeys and they looked at it. Very carefully, they walked over to see what the light was. Like all Glowmen, Lummp was very good with animals. They loved him and he loved them.

The donkeys were not afraid of Lummp. They walked over to stand next to him. He reached out his arm and took the bag off the donkey. The key was inside the bag! He gave it to Ari and Ari quickly unlocked the cage.

The guards were taking a nap. Ari and Denza quietly took their weapons and gave them to other Sliwohs. They gathered all the donkeys and slowly walked away from the cage. They were very quiet as they escaped Spring Field.

Tomorrow, they would take the long way around Hill Side, and then would return to Bird's Field. Ari, Denza, and Luump would tell the others what had happened, then they would take back the other kidnapped Sliwohs to their towns too.

Soon, all of the Sliwoh towns would unite. Soon they would join together to create an army. They would fight the miners...and the humans too if they saw any.

The innocent Sliwohs had learned two important lessons. The world is a very scary place...and never trust a human!

Annex to Chapter 3

Summary

Ari and the others arrive in the Western sea town of Spring Field. It is a very beautiful town, but there is something wrong about it. Soon, Ari learns Yardum's secret- -he has been working with the miners! The humans sold Denza, Ari, and Lummp as slaves, but Lummp helped them escape the evil town and return to Bird's Field.

Multiple-choice questions
Select one answer for each question

11. Spring Field is a:
    a. mountain town
    b. Sliwoh town
    c. human town
    d. sea town

12. Yardum sold the Sliwoh's to the miners. What else did he sell?
    a. Some horses
    b. Some blankets
    c. A stolen crown
    d. Weapons

13. The miners make very good:
    a. guns
    b. jewels
    c. soup
    d. cabins

14. Lummp saw the miner put a key:

a. in a bag on a donkey
b. in a blanket on a horse
c. in another miner's pocket
d. in Sadida's hand

15. When the Sliwohs returned home, they:
    a. had a dance
    b. ate a large meal
    c. joined with other Sliwoh towns
    d. killed all humans

11. d
12. c
13. a
14. a
15. c

4. My Friend, The Supercomputer

Chapter 1

"Congratulations, Thom," the French doctor said to me.

She was young for a doctor. I thought she looked very smart. I also thought she was very attractive.

"The operation was a success," she said, smiling at me. "Your brain is now linked to our supercomputer."

"Oh," I said. I felt tired. It had been a long operation. "Can I have a drink?"

"Not yet, Thom. How do you feel?"

"I'm thirsty," I said. "But, I feel good. It's funny, but I don't feel any pain." I was lying on a bed at the hospital in Switzerland. There were three people in the small room...and one giant black computer. The computer was bigger than a refrigerator.

It was supercomputer--the fastest, smartest computer in all of Europe.

The name of the computer was Titan 2035 (2035 was the year is had been built) and I was now connected to it.

"Of course, you do not feel pain. The human brain cannot feel pain," the French doctor said. Her name was Doctor Sheila Benoit. She was one ~f ~¹ 2035. "Relax now. We will start the c

I looked at the large compute knowledge than all the libraries on Ear 2035, my brain seemed very small an information will you download?" I ask

"All of it!" said Doctor Benoit's assistant, Professor Bidwell. He was much older than her, and with a white beard and reading glasses. "Why wait? Your mind can handle it all!"

"No, don't listen to him. He is joking," Benoit said. "Of course, we will be very careful. We will download as much data as possible. But, we cannot do all of it in one day."

"Would it kill me?" I asked. "Or could my mind really handle it all?"

Professor Bidwell looked at the young doctor, then at me. "I don't think it would kill you, but that is my opinion, and I am not in charge."

"No, it would not kill you, Thom," Benoit agreed. "But, it might make you crazy. We do not know how much information your mind can take, so we will go slowly. We will not hurt you, I promise." She smiled and patted me on the head. "You are too expensive. We don't want to damage you."

*

The process of the data link began. The information slowly leaked from Titan 2035 to my brain. At first, I did not notice it, but then I became aware of the new facts and the new information. It was transferred to my long term memory. The information was new, but it seemed like I had known it for a long time.

They were feeding me different types of information: mathematics, history, science, technologies. I was also learning medicine, law enforcement procedures, fighting tactics, acting techniques...a lot of variety!

Three hours passed. Doctor Benoit and Professor Bidwell were sitting quietly the whole time. The third person the room was an investor. He was very old and he wore an

84

expensive silver suit. When he walked, he used a cane to help him.

I knew he was the owner of TRANSMUTE Corporation. His Swiss company owned the hospital. It had paid for the supercomputer...and for the operation.

"Are you almost finished, Sheila?" he asked. "You said three hours." He pointed to a clock on the wall. "It has been three hours."

"Yes sir," she said. "I will end the download process soon, then we will disconnect him from the computer."

"When will the tests be finished?" the investor asked. He had spent millions of Euros in research and development. He was eager to learn the results of this experiment.

"We will test Thom tonight and tomorrow. If his brain has accepted the information we downloaded, he should be able to pass the tests," Doctor Benoit said.

"Then, we will link him up again," Professor Bidwell said. "We will transfer more data tomorrow or the next day."

"Excellent," the investor said. He stood up to leave. "Good job, Thom," he said to me.

"Thank you," I said. For some reason, I could not remember his name. It was very strange because I knew the name of his company. "I'm sorry, but I don't know your name."

"That is alright," he said, walking out of the room. "You don't need to know it anymore."

Doctor Benoit watched him leave. When he was gone, she turned to the professor.

"Are you ready to begin the disconnect process?" she asked.

"Are you sure you don't want to give Thom a little more?"

She shook her head. "He has had enough. Let's turn off the data stream."

*

I felt myself getting sleepy. Everything went black. I do not know how long I was asleep.

My dreams were long and unpleasant...dreams of war and suffering, and of death and destruction. There was no way to tell how long I was asleep.

I finally woke up and opened my eyes. Above me, I could see the sky and the clouds.

That's funny. Am I still dreaming? I wondered. *Where is the ceiling?*

Then, I turned my head and saw the room. It had been destroyed. Quickly, I sat up and looked around. Doctor Benoit was on the floor dead. Professor Bidwell was missing. The black supercomputer, Titan 2035, was alright. It was still turned on and feeding me information!

But, the rest of the hospital was gone. A massive bomb had exploded and destroyed the hospital as I had slept. Far away, I heard someone yelling for help. Further away, I heard the sound of police cars coming.

There was a terrorist attack, I thought. *Or did this happen because of me? Did somebody try to kill me?*

Whoever did this made a big mistake, I decided, slowly getting off my bed. I unhooked myself from Titan 2035. *I'm not dead and I will find out who did this...and make them pay!*

Summary

Thom is connected to a supercomputer. His doctor and her assistant are transferring information from the computer, Titan 2035, to Thom's brain. There is also an investor in the room, but he leaves before they are finished. Thom goes to sleep. When he wakes up, he sees the hospital has been destroyed and his doctor is dead.

Multiple-choice questions
Select one answer for each question

1. How many people are in the room, including Thom?
   a. 2
   b. 3
   c. 4
   d. 5

2. Where did Titan 2035 get part of its name?
   a. Its serial number
   b. The year it was built
   c. The current year
   d. None of the above

3. What reason does Doctor Benoit gives for wanting to be careful?
   a. They spent a lot of money on Thom
   b. They spent a lot of money on Titan
   c. She is in love with Thom
   d. Her assistant tells her to slow down

4. Why do they want to stop after three hours?
   a. Thom would get bored
   b. Thom would be tired
   c. Too much information could be dangerous for Thom
   d. Too much information could make Thom sleepy

5. At first, what does Thom think happened to the hospital?
   a. A gas explosion
   b. A fire
   c. An accident
   d. A terrorist attack

1. c
2. b
3. a
4. c
5. d

Chapter 2

"What do you remember about the explosion, Mister Parmenter?"

"I already told you," I said, sitting at the police station. We were in a small room with a large mirror. There was a metal table between me and the police officer. "Call me Thom. And I don't remember anything because I was asleep."

The blonde policewoman was recording our conversation. In her ear was a microphone. Someone was telling her what to ask me. Someone sitting on the other side of the mirror, perhaps.

"Do you have any idea who blew up the hospital?" she asked. Her Swiss accent was very strong, but her English grammar was good. "Any idea at all?"

I looked at the camera that was recording me. "Police should not be playing guessing games," I said. "Do I have an idea? Of course. It was the owner of the company."

"What company?" she asked. "TRANSMUTE Corporation?"

"Right. What other company is there? I'm talking about the owner of the company which paid for the experiment."

The policewoman stared at me. "That does not make sense. Why would he destroy his own work?"

"How do you know the owner is a man?" I asked. "You said 'he.'"

She blinked her eyes. She ignored my question. "Do you think it is a coincidence that you lived, but the others died?"

"I don't think it was an accident," I said, standing up. "I don't believe in coincidence. A bomb destroyed a whole hospital, but I lived. I believe that was on purpose."

I was finished with the interview. The female officer asked me to sit down. I refused.

"I said sit down, Mister Parmenter..."

"Call me Thom," I said, walking over to the mirror. "There are three people sitting on the other side of this mirror. One of them works for TRANSMUTE. He is telling you what to ask me."

"Why do you say that?" she asked. But, her face told me everything I needed to know. Her expression told me the truth.

"I'm leaving," I said. "The interview is over. Open the door."

"Thom, we still have some questions to ask you--"

"No, you don't. You are asking questions that you know the answers to." The door was locked. There was an electronic keypad by the door. Without thinking, I punched in the code and the door unlocked. "You know who blew up the building. And you know why he did it."

She did not try to stop me from leaving. "Why?" she asked.

I turned and pointed at my head. "To create me."

*

There was a news station across town. I got in a taxi and told him to take me there.

The media was happy to meet with me. We set up a fast press conference. Many news stations and magazines sent reporters. I gave all of them a fantastic story free of charge.

"You don't want money for your story?" they asked. It was hard for them to believe.

"I only want the truth to be told to the public. People must know the truth! The owner of TRANSMUTE wanted to kill my doctor. He wanted to make it look like a terrorist attack, but it was him."

"But, why would he do that?"

"So the experiment would never end. I was connected to the supercomputer for many hours, much longer than I was supposed to be. My doctor, Doctor Benoit, wanted to be careful. She wanted to download small amounts of data."

"But you think--"

"I don't 'think.' I know. I know the owner wanted to keep me hooked up longer. He and Professor Bidwell wanted to push me. To see how much information a human mind can hold."

"How much can it hold?" the reporter asked me.

I smiled at the reporter. "Too much," I said.

The reporter's name was Michael James Beckett, and he was married with one daughter. I knew his age, his address, and his parents' names and address. I knew where he graduated college, what his grades were, and who all of his social media friends were.

I told him his car's license plate number and how many traffic violations he'd gotten last year. I also told him to stop smoking.

"How do you know I smoke?" he asked.

"It's in your medical files."

*

The owner of the company was not arrested. There was no proof that he had anything to do with the explosion. He even asked to meet me privately.

"Son, you can't go around making these wild accusations," he said, offering me a drink.

"Keep your drink. I don't trust you."

"Fine," he said, sitting down. "But if you say another word about me, I will sue you."

"Go ahead, I don't have any money," I said. But, I knew he was lying. He wouldn't sue me. He would probably have me killed instead. "It's funny. I know almost everything about everyone, but I cannot remember your name. Even when people tell me, I forget it. Why is that?"

"I would not know," he said with a shrug. "Maybe it is a glitch. Some kind of error in your brain function. With so much new information inside your head, you will probably forget some things."

"Yeah. Too bad my doctor is dead, huh?"

"Look, Thom...I told you. I had nothing to do with it. Stop blaming me."

"And where is Professor Bidwell?" I asked. "His body was never found."

"That is a good question," he said, as he poured a glass of water. "The police told me they are looking for him. Here, at least drink some water."

I looked at the glass. He really wanted me to have it. "Okay," I said, taking it from him with my left hand. He stood up a little to hand it to me.

I slipped my left foot behind him, like a hook. With my right hand, I pushed his face as hard as I could. He tripped backward and fell hard.

I jumped on him, pouring the water in his open mouth. He tried to spit it out, but I held his mouth closed. He swallowed it.

His body shook for a few minutes, then stopped moving forever.

"Funny," I said. "People always say to drink more water, but look what happens when you do."

Annex to Chapter 2

Summary

Thom meets with news reporters. He tells them that he thinks the owner of TRANSMUTE Corporation caused the hospital explosion. The owner meets Thom too. He threatens to sue Thom. He offers Thom a glass of poisoned water, but Thom makes him drink it instead.

Multiple-choice questions
Select one answer for each question

6. Why does Thom speak to reporters?
    a. To sell his story for money
    b. To become famous
    c. To meet the owner of TRANSMUTE
    d. To tell the public the truth about the explosion

7. How does Thom know everything about the reporter?
    a. Because Thom downloaded so much information
    b. Because Thom read the man's files during lunch
    c. Because Thom knows the man from college
    d. None of the above

8. What does Thom think about Professor Bidwell?
    a. That he's working in Brazil
    b. That he's working for Titan 2035
    c. That he's dead
    d. That he's working with the owner of TRANSMUTE

9. Why does the owner want Thom to drink something?
    a. Because Thom is thirsty
    b. Because Thom feels tired

c. Because he wants to poison Thom

d. Because he wants to sue Thom

10. How does Thom get the owner to drink the water?

    a. He tricks the owner

    b. They both drink some water

    c. Thom switches their glasses

    d. Thom pours the water in his mouth

6. d
7. a
8. d
9. c
10. d

Chapter 3

Great. Now the police are after me.

I didn't mean to kill the TRANSMUTE Corporation's owner. All I did was make him drink his own water. Does that make me the bad guy?

It doesn't matter. I am on the run now. The police are after me.

I tried to tell the world what had happened to me...but I never got to finish my story.

I never got to tell them that I'm not a human anymore.

The transfer of information with Titan 2035 changed me. I am exactly what TRANSMUTE wanted. I'm a "transhuman."

My doctor is dead. I have no way to undo what they did. The only person who might be able to help is Professor Bidwell. He is still missing, but perhaps I will be able to find him.

I am pretty smart these days!

In fact, I am now the smartest living creature on Earth (I don't count Titan, it isn't alive).

*

In the end, it only took me two days to find Bidwell. He was hiding on the Pacific island of Guam. It is a good hiding place since it is so far away from Europe...but it is a very small island. Once you are there, there is no place to run.

"How much did he pay you?" I asked, sitting on Bidwell's chest.

"Get off of me," he said. "I can't breathe."

"If you are speaking, you must be able to breathe," I argued. "Now talk!"

"You want to know about Zafer?"

"Is that the owner of TRANSMUTE? His name is Zafer?"

"Yes, but you will forget his name. He doesn't want you to know who he is."

"I don't think he will care now," I said. "The man is dead."

Bidwell looked shocked. "You killed him?"

My feet were crushing his wrists, but I pushed down more. He cried out.

"I didn't kill anyone. He gave me a glass of water. I made him drink it. It must've been poisoned."

"Then you killed him," the professor said. "Don't make excuses! You're a murderer!"

"And so are you!" I said, standing up. "You helped him blow up the hospital. Didn't you?"

"No," he said. "I swear, I did not know he would do that."

"But you disappeared. You weren't there when the place exploded."

"He had left. Then, he called me to meet him outside." Bidwell was trying to sit up. He was breathing hard. "I left to meet him, and that is when the hospital blew up. I ran away. I was scared."

"Scared of what?"

"I was scared the police would blame me. Like you are blaming me now!"

"Well, it does look suspicious. You ran away from a crime."

At last, the old professor stood up on weak knees. He searched around the floor for his glasses. I was holding them.

"I need those," he said.

"I need to know how to undo the experiment," I said. "I don't want to be this intelligent. I can't think for myself, there is too much information in my brain. I have no thoughts of my own. I am not a real person anymore."

"Many people would love to have what you have," he said. "Including me."

"That is because you don't have it," I said. "If you were like me, you would understand. It is awful. Doctor Benoit was right. It should have been done a little at a time."

He sighed. "What do you want from me, Thom? What is done is done. The laboratory is destroyed and all the equipment and all the research is destroyed. Sheila is dead. We cannot go back in time."

"Not all of the equipment is destroyed," I said, giving him his glasses. "Titan 2035 was not damaged."

"Then perhaps you should be talking to it, instead of me."

"That's funny," I said, turning to leave. "I was just thinking the same thing."

     *

The plane ride from Guam back to Switzerland was very long, but I was happy to get back. I was travelling under a false identity, so the police would not track me. When I returned, I went looking for Titan 2035. They had moved it from the ruined hospital, of course, but I knew where it would be--inside the TRANSMUTE Corporation building.

I waited until night, then I broke into the building. Titan was locked in a secured room, but I easily got inside. I turned on the computer system and began speaking to Titan in its own language--computer code.

"Professor Bidwell said something interesting," I told Titan. "He said, you cannot go back in time."

"Incorrect," Titan stated. "It is simple to travel back and forth through spacetime."

"I know that now, but there is a part I am still confused about. I need your help, Titan..."

*

Together, we worked out the mathematics for engineering a time machine. It wasn't hard, but there were parts my organic brain could not figure out, and Titan had trouble with some of the more creative thinking parts, but we worked as a team and solved the riddle.

Bidwell, of course, was wrong. The research about my connection to Titan was never destroyed...because Titan had it all stored inside itself. And that was the key to travelling back in time.

I reconnected my mind to Titan, but this time, instead of downloading data from it, I would upload myself to Titan.

So, that is what we did.

The only problem? Once I was merged with Titan 2035, I didn't want to go back. I didn't want to change the past. I didn't want to be just "Thom Parmenter" anymore because now, I wasn't even a transhuman, I was something more.

Something I cannot explain to you...because you are still just a human.

But don't worry. Titan and I have a solution to your problem. We can fix you.

Today, you are only human, but you won't be for much longer!

Annex to Chapter 3

Summary

Thom finds Professor Bidwell who is hiding on an island, but Thom learns nothing new. He goes back to look for Titan 2035. Together, they discover a method for time travel. But instead of going back in time, Thom changes his mind. He decides to change other humans, to make them like he is.

Multiple-choice questions
Select one answer for each question

11. Professor Bidwell was hiding:
    a. on an island near Europe
    b. on a boat
    c. in a mountain cabin
    d. on an island in the Pacific Ocean

12. Was Bidwell working for Zafer?
    a. Yes, they blew up the hospital together
    b. Yes, but Bidwell did not help blow up the hospital
    c. It is not clear
    d. No

13. Thom left Bidwell alone because:
    a. Bidwell could not help him
    b. Bidwell pointed a gun at him
    c. Bidwell tried to poison him
    d. Bidwell wanted to help him

14. What did Titan 2035 think about time travel?
    a. It is impossible

b. It has been done before

c. It is possible with a black hole

d. It is simple

15. Why did Thom change his mind about time travel?
    a. He was afraid to change the past
    b. He was afraid to change the future
    c. He wanted to make everyone else like him
    d. He died

11. d
12. b
13. a
14. d
15. c

This title is also available as an audiobook.

For more information, please visit the Amazon store.

5. The Town of Skull Tooth

Chapter 1

The Old West was famous for its bloody history. Deadwood, South Dakota; San Antonio, Texas; Tombstone, Arizona...there were many dangerous, lawless towns. In some cases, the town sheriff was the most powerful person. He maintained law and order.

But, not every town had a sheriff.

Skull Tooth, Oklahoma, for example! Skull Tooth had no sheriff, no laws, and no rules. It was not civilized at all. Everyone did what they wanted.

Gambling, fighting, drinking, and other vices took place all day and all night, seven days a week. Most days, somebody was murdered before breakfast. Or during breakfast!

Yet the town continued to grow every year. And every year, a new criminal would arrive and try to take control. They would try to become the boss of Skull Tooth, the boss of everyone who lived there.

To control the crime, you had to be tougher than the other criminals. To make money, you had to want it more than the others.

That is why the bosses never lived long. They were always killed and replaced!

Until one late autumn day, Erkek Tex came to town.

The people who lived there, the citizens of Skull Tooth, knew he was bad news. They could tell when he rode his horse into town. His horse was pale, whiter than a sheet. His face was tough like leather, his skin tanned from the sun.

Under his nose was a giant black moustache. The moustache dropped down past his lips. His eyebrows were as bushy as his moustache.

"Where do you think that man came from?" a store owner asked his friend. His friend owned the bar across the street. The bar was named The Windy Plains Saloon.

"He is not from around here," said the bar owner. "He looks like a foreigner."

"Well Marty, what country do you think he's from?"

Marty raised his hands. He didn't know.

The store owner looked at Erkek Tex. Tex was tying his white horse to a post. The sun was setting and the wind had turned cold. Tex took out a small container. He took some tobacco from it and rolled a cigarette. He bent his head to light the cigarette. His large brown cowboy hat covered his eyes.

When he looked back up, Tex was looking at Marty, the bar owner. "Who is watching your bar, if you are sitting over there?" he asked. His accent was very thick, he sounded like he was from the Middle East. He would never tell anyone in town, but his family had emigrated from the Ottoman Empire. In fact, his nickname, "Erkek," meant "man" in Turkish.

"I try to stay outside," Marty said. "In my bar, customers take what they want, and they pay what they want. Otherwise, there is trouble."

"What do you mean, 'trouble?'"

"I mean, they have shot the last three owners of The Windy Plains Saloon."

"Go back to your bar," Erkek Tex said. "I am going inside. And I don't like to pour my own drinks."

The bar owner looked at Tex. Tex was not a large man, but he wasn't too small. He had some muscles, but his body was lean. There were guns on both of his hips.

"Stranger," Marty said, "I will go over there, but don't start shooting people. I don't want any trouble."

"I don't want any trouble either," Tex said. "That is why there will not be any."

The bar owner who was also the bartender--the man who served drinks--walked across the street. Inside The Windy Plains Saloon there were a dozen men. Some of them were playing a game of cards. Some were sitting in chairs at tables, holding glasses or bottles. A few were sitting at the long wooden bar counter talking in loud voices. When they saw the bar owner walk in, they stopped.

"Get out of here, Marty!" said one of the men at the bar counter. He was tall and had curly brown hair and a brown beard. His clothes were torn and he smelled terrible. He stood up from his stool. "We're putting our money on the counter. We're taking what we want to drink, so we don't need you."

"That's alright," the bar owner said, "I just came to check on things."

The curly-haired man whose nickname was "Curly" walked over. He put his hand on Marty's chest. "I said, we don't need you. There is nothing for you to check on. You can leave now."

Curly's friend laughed. "Yeah, leave us alone you old man!"

Marty frowned and turned to go back out. But then, Erkek Tex walked through the doors.

Tex looked at the man with curly hair. "Bartender," said Tex in a very deep voice, "I have ridden many miles today. I'm very thirsty. Stop standing around and go get me a drink."

Curly spit on the floor. "I am not the bartender!"

"Then where is the bartender? I am tired of waiting!"

Curly pointed at Marty. "This is the bartender, but we don't want him in here."

"That is fine," Tex said. "If he is leaving, then you can get my drink. Now!"

Curly pulled out his gun and pointed it at Erkek Tex. "Nobody talks to me like--"

The sound of a gun firing echoed in the bar. Curly fell to the ground dead.

"Who is going to be the bartender?" Tex asked, with the gun in his hand smoking.

Everyone pointed at Marty.

Summary

The town of Skull Tooth, Oklahoma is very dangerous because there is no sheriff. No one is in charge. A mysterious cowboy named Erkek Tex comes to town. He asks Marty, the owner of the town's bar, to go inside the bar. Tex walks in. He sees the customers do not want Marty there. One of the customers points a gun at Tex, but Tex kills him first.

Multiple-choice questions
Select one answer for each question

1. Erkek Tex's family came from:
   a. Oklahoma
   b. Mexico
   c. Deadwood, South Dakota
   d. Ottoman Empire

2. Marty owns the town:
   a. store
   b. horse stable
   c. bar
   d. barber shop

3. What colour is Tex's horse?
   a. White
   b. Brown
   c. Black
   d. Dark grey

4. Why does Marty sit outside?
    a. He trusts his customers
    b. He is afraid of his customers
    c. He doesn't have any customers
    d. Someone else is helping the customers

5. What does Curly want?
    a. To pour Tex a drink
    b. For Marty to leave
    c. For Marty to pour Tex a drink
    d. To kill Marty and Tex

Answers to Chapter 1

1. d
2. c
3. a
4. b
5. b

Chapter 2

"This town is not big enough for both of us," said "Daring Diablo" Noel Cruz. Daring Diablo was an outlaw from the state of Texas. He was wanted by the police in several states. They wanted to capture him for many different crimes.

If you saw a "WANTED" poster with his face, the poster usually said "Dead or Alive."

Daring Diablo was tired of running from the law, so he had gone somewhere the law did not exist. He had moved to Skull Tooth, Oklahoma.

In Skull Tooth, he was able to make a nice living. He managed some card games, and he bought and sold gold. Sometimes, he helped smuggle weapons up from Mexico. It was a good life. He was free from fear. He did not worry about police knocking on his door.

But sometimes, strangers came to town. They wanted to take over. They wanted to be a big boss. They wanted to make trouble. Daring Diablo did not like that. He didn't want someone in charge of the town. If someone were in charge, things would become organized. If things became too organized, it would attract attention.

Nobody in Oklahoma cared about Skull Tooth. Everyone left the place alone. It was too small for the police to bother with, but if someone started making a lot of money, more people would move there. It was already growing faster than Daring Diablo wanted.

"We have to deal with this new character," he said to his wife. She was a Native American woman from the Cherokee Indian tribe. Her name was Ayita, which meant "first the dance."

They lived together in a small log cabin. The cabin was on the edge of town. They owned several acres of land. Nobody ever came to visit them.

But sometimes, they would go into town for supplies. They knew the town had been changing. They had seen it growing quickly, and they knew it was because of the stranger--Erkek Tex.

"Leave Erkek Tex alone," she said, as she cooked some stew. "He has only been here for four months. Soon, he will become tired of this place. He will leave."

"I don't think so," Daring Diablo said, cleaning his rifle. Most of the criminals in town liked to carry guns. Most carried handguns. Handguns or pistols were smaller and easier to walk around with, but Daring Diablo did not care. A long rifle was more powerful. He was fast with his rifle. He was as fast with his rifle as most were with their handguns.

But, he never used his weapon unless he had to. He didn't want to kill anybody.

When you kill a person, there is always trouble, he thought. *Some relative of the dead person will come. They will try to shoot you. Or the police come looking for you...*

"Tex is a little bit like me," he said. "He likes it here, out in the open fields. No one around, and nobody bothers you here. But, he is like the others too. He wants to make a name for himself. He wants to rule this town."

Ayita used a large spoon to scoop some of the stew into a bowl. It was very hot. She put the stew on the table. "Eat your dinner," she said.

"I'm not hungry."

"Put down your rifle," she said. "It is clean enough. You never use it. Come eat."

Daring Diablo dropped his cleaning cloth and put the rifle down. He got up from his chair and went to the table.

"Listen to me, woman. I know what I'm talking about. That Ottoman Turk has big plans for this place. He's got people working for him. New businesses have opened up. Soon, the town will be twice as big, then the police will start coming to Skull Tooth. Someone will notice there isn't a sheriff."

She put down a bowl of hot stew for herself, then she brought over some bread. "Maybe you could be the sheriff."

He laughed. "Me? I am a wanted man. The police are after me. I am wanted for many crimes!"

"Then you need to stay hidden. Don't make a problem with the stranger."

Daring Diablo tore a piece of bread and dipped it in his stew. "That stranger already made the problem," he said. "And tonight, I am going to fix it."

*

Daring Diablo took his rifle and a bag. He got on his horse and rode into town. Most of the citizens of Skull Tooth were indoors. The night was cold, he could see his breath in the air.

"Where is Erkek Tex?" he asked a person on the street. The person was wearing an expensive jacket and new boots.

"Who wants to know?" the person asked, looking at Daring Diablo. Diablo knew most of the people in town. He did not recognize this stranger.

More and more new people, he thought. *This growth has to stop!*

"If you do not know my name," Diablo said, "then you must be new here."

"Maybe I am, maybe I'm not," said the man in the fancy jacket. "But I asked you a question. Who are you?"

Daring Diablo was shocked. No one in Skull Tooth had ever spoken to him like this! "I'm Noel Cruz. Folks call me 'Daring Diablo.'"

"That is a stupid nickname. If you don't know where Tex is, you don't need to know. Good evening!" The man kicked a rock and walked away.

Diablo wanted to jump off his horse and hit the man, but he took a deep breath and looked around. The Windy Plains Saloon was well-lit. He heard voices coming from inside. Since he was in town, he might as well get a drink.

"Look who is here!" someone shouted when Diablo walked into the bar. "Come sit down with us!" The man who had shouted waved to Diablo. He was sitting at a table full of men.

Diablo sat down.

"Why did you come into town tonight?" they asked him.

Diablo ordered a drink from Marty and told them his plan.

After he told them, Diablo said, "Now I only need to know two things. Where is Erkek Tex? And, who wants to help me kill him?"

Annex to Chapter 2

Summary

Noel Cruz, also known as Daring Diablo, is a criminal. He is hiding in Skull Tooth because no police ever go there. He doesn't want the town to get bigger. He doesn't like Erkek Tex because Tex is making the town grow. Diablo's wife wants him to leave Tex alone, but Diablo goes into town to look for Tex. He goes to the bar and meets some men.

Multiple-choice questions
Select one answer for each question

6. Where does Diablo live?
    a. In a wooden cabin near town
    b. In a house in the middle of town
    c. In the town next to Skull Tooth
    d. With his wife, in Texas

7. What does Ayita want?
    a. She wants her husband to kill Erkek Tex
    b. She wants to go to town
    c. She wants her husband to leave Tex alone
    d. She wants to move to Nevada

8. What kind of gun does Diablo like to use?
    a. He uses a rifle
    b. He uses a pistol
    c. He doesn't use guns
    d. He uses a machine gun

9. Why is Diablo shocked after talking to a man on the street?

a. The man is wearing funny clothes
b. The man is a stranger and he speaks rudely to Diablo
c. The man makes fun of Diablo's rifle
d. The man want to dance with Diablo's wife

10. How many men does Diablo meet inside the bar?
    a. 2
    b. 4
    c. 5
    d. It doesn't say how many

6. a
7. c
8. a
9. b
10. d

Chapter 3

"This town is not big enough for both of us. You have to leave," Daring Diablo said, "or die." He was carrying his rifle. He raised it up in the air.

Erkek Tex was sitting in a barber chair. He was having his hair cut and his moustache trimmed. The barber, an overweight man with red cheeks, stopped cutting.

"I did not say to stop working," Tex told the man. So, the barber went back to work, but kept one eye on Diablo.

"Hey!" Daring Diablo yelled. "Did you hear me?"

"You are very persistent, Noel Cruz," Tex said, calling Diablo by his real name. "That can get a man into trouble."

"I did not come to argue. I came to make you leave."

Tex raised his hand for the barber to stop. He whispered something to the barber, and the man left. Then, Erkek Tex got out of the chair. He brushed his large black moustache with a small comb. He always carried a moustache comb. He liked to look good, especially for his enemies.

Diablo was confused. Why was Tex so calm? Diablo pointed his rifle at Tex who slowly began walking to the door.

"You are right!" Tex said loudly. He walked outside. "I say, you're right, Daring Diablo! Skull Tooth is not big enough for me! So, it cannot be big enough for me and you!"

A small crowd had already begun to gather. The barber had been telling people to come outside. Tex spoke to the crowd of people.

Diablo was not alone, though. He had two friends hiding. His friends were also carrying weapons. If Erkek Tex tried anything, the three of them would shoot Tex down.

But, the Ottoman Turk wasn't stupid. He put on his cowboy hat and kept his hands up. He did not reach for his pistols.

"I want you out of here!" Diablo shouted. "We all want you to leave Skull Tooth. We want things to go back to the way they were!"

"Is that right?" Tex asked. "If that's true, then okay. You stay here, Noel Cruz. Stay here, so the police can't find you! Stay here and do nothing! I do not judge you and I do not blame you!"

"I told you once, Tex," Diablo said. "I didn't come to argue!" He kept the barrel of his rifle pointed at Tex's chest. "Don't make me have to shoot you."

"No, no, I won't! I can promise you that! I never give anybody a reason to shoot me," Tex said, looking around at the crowd. "That is not my style. I try to be good to people! I try to bring in some new business – some new money – but I don't try to pick fights. I hate fighting!"

"You shot Curly on your first day here! Everyone knows that."

"Yes, I did!" Tex admitted. "But I did not start that fight. I was protecting myself, and a man has a right to do that! Doesn't he?"

The people in the crowd nodded. One of them shouted, "Tex is right!"

Diablo knew Tex was not telling the truth. He had not been defending himself against Curly. He had started the fight, then he shot Curly dead. But, that didn't matter now.

"I'm going to count to ten, Tex. You better get going!"

"Okay, I already agreed with you," Tex said. "You stay here! I will go pack my bags!" Tex took one last look into the crowd. A few of his friends were there. "I'm leaving, boys! Don't try to stop me!"

"No, don't go," said one of the men. "You've been a good boss!"

"Yes, the best boss!" said another one of the criminals. "Skull Tooth needs you!"

"I know, I know, but look, Mister Darling Diablo here--"

"'Daring,' not 'Darling!'" Diablo said.

"Sorry. Mister Diablo wants me gone. He wants to be in charge. It is his turn now!"

"That's not what I said," Diablo protested. "I don't want to be in charge--"

"Fight him, Tex!" a woman in the crowd yelled. It was one of Tex's girlfriends. "You are faster than him."

Daring Diablo was getting nervous. He did not expect the people of Skull Tooth to act this way. He thought they hated Tex as much as he did, but they were acting like he was their best friend.

Tex nodded, but looked at Diablo. "I am the fastest gun in Oklahoma. That's a fact! But, Noel Cruz has brought friends with him." He pointed to one of Diablo's friends who was hiding on a rooftop. "He has outsmarted me. He's your boss now! He earned it!"

"People, that's not what I want!" Diablo shouted to the crowd. "I'm not here to take over. I don't want Skull Tooth to grow too much. That will bring a sheriff here! That will bring law here!"

Marty the bartender had been watching. Now, he walked out to stand next to Erkek Tex. "We already have law here. Tex's law!"

The crowd began to shout and clap.

Marty continued. "Tex, what can we do to make you stay?"

Erkek Tex shrugged his shoulders. "There is only one thing I can think of! If Noel Cruz, also known as the outlaw Daring Diablo, did not exist...I would not have this problem!"

Tex looked up at the rooftop. The man who had been up there was gone, and Tex knew the other gunman was gone too.

Daring Diablo was alone.

"If I didn't exist?" Diablo said. He was getting scared, but he still had his rifle. He kept it pointed at Tex. "Then you have a problem, Tex. I do exist!"

A second later, several guns fired. Noel Cruz, the "Daring Diablo" from Texas, fell dead in the middle of the street. Tex looked down at the dead man's body.

"No, you don't exist," he said. "Not in my town."

Annex to Chapter 3

Summary

Daring Diablo finds Erkek Tex in a barbershop. He tells Tex to leave town. Tex walks outside and begins talking. People from town have come to listen. Diablo has two friends hiding, but they leave. They leave because the people of Skull Tooth want Tex to stay. So, they kill Daring Diablo.

Multiple-choice questions
Select one answer for each question

11. What is Tex doing in the barbershop?
    a. Getting his hair and moustache cut
    b. Getting his beard shaved off
    c. Getting his hair shaved off
    d. Getting his fingernails cut

12. Who asks Tex to stay?
    a. The barbershop owner
    b. The bar owner
    c. The store owner
    d. Tex's girlfriend

13. Why did Tex leave the barbershop to go outside?
    a. To get some fresh air
    b. To look for his girlfriend
    c. So the people could listen to him
    d. So the barber could finish cutting his hair

14. What reason does Tex give for killing Curly?
    a. He said Curly was cheating at cards
    b. He said he was defending himself from Curly

c. He said he was protecting Marty from Curly

d. He said Curly had shot the store owner

15. Who kills Daring Diablo?

    a. Erkek Tex

    b. Ayita

    c. Marty

    d. The people of Skull Tooth

11. a
12. b
13. c
14. b
15. d

6. The Church

Chapter 1

The bus driver kept looking at Amber. He was staring at her using his rear-view mirror. She noticed that he had been doing it for a while. It was really starting to bother her.

Amber looked around at the empty seats on the bus. It was a large city bus. She was the last passenger on it. The city was asleep. It was almost two o'clock in the morning.

He keeps looking at me, Amber thought. *I guess he thinks I'm very pretty. But, he looks like a hairy caveman.*

She tried to ignore him. She gazed out of her window into the darkness. They passed by dark buildings. Every building had its lights off. And, there were almost no other cars on the road...

Suddenly, she realized, *I don't know which road we are on! This is not the street we should be on.*

Alarmed, Amber turned her head and saw the bus driver. He was driving and smiling at nothing.

What is this guy doing??

She got out of her seat, holding her small purse. The bus ride had been very smooth, but when she started walking toward the front, one of the bus's wheels hit a hole in the road. Amber fell forward. She reached out her arm. She grabbed a seat back and caught herself from falling.

The bus driver laughed.

He drove into that pothole on purpose!

"Sit down, little lady!" the driver said. He had to take deep breaths after each sentence. He had some breathing problem. "We're on a rocky road now!"

"Excuse me, but which road are we on?" she asked. "Are you lost?"

"What do you mean? I never get lost!" He took a deep breath and laughed with his mouth opened wide. He was missing several teeth. He scratched at his beard and coughed. "I told you to sit down. It isn't safe to stand up while the bus is moving. We don't want you to hurt your pretty head. It might mess up your hairdo!"

Amber did not think the situation was funny. She had heard of things like this happening. But, she was not scared, not yet. She held her purse tighter and walked closer to the driver.

"Tell me where are you going? I do not recognize this road. This isn't the right way."

"It's right for me," the driver said mysteriously. Instead of looking at her in the mirror, he turned his head to stare at her. There were cookie crumbs in his beard. His eyes were red and bloodshot. Even from her distance away from him, Amber could smell him.

Did this guy take a shower this year? He really stinks!

Without warning, the bus driver reached out at her. Amber stepped backward, and he laughed again.

"I'm just messing with you," he said, breathing heavily. "Stop worrying, I am a professional. I know what I am doing."

Amber did not like this. She sat down and waited, wondering if she should make a phone call. *He is acting weird,* she thought, *but maybe he really is lost. Sometimes, new drivers forget the roads. Maybe, he does not want to admit he is lost. He does not know where we are, but he feels embarrassed.*

The driver began to slow down. Amber peeked out of the window. She did not see any street lights or stop signs. *Why is he slowing down? Will he turn the bus around?*

"Almost there," he said. He took a drink from a plastic bottle. Amber did not think it was water inside the bottle.

The bus pulled into a large, unused parking lot. The lot was empty; there were no other cars in it. There was grass growing from cracks in the lot. There were broken glass bottles and pieces of litter everywhere. A stray dog was walking around.

The parking lot was dark; there were no street lights. The driver stopped and removed his seat belt.

"Last stop," he said. He took another drink and wiped his lips on his shirt sleeve. "Time for all pretty girls to get off my bus."

Amber stood up. He opened the bus door and pointed to it.

She shook her head. "This isn't my stop. What do you think you are doing?"

"You will find out soon," he said. "Get off the bus."

She took out her phone, but there was no time. He moved toward her fast.

Amber pressed the call button, but it dialled the last person she'd called--her sister!

"Hi, Sis," said Amber's sister, Aisha. "Do you know how late it is?"

The driver knocked the phone out of Amber's hand.

"Help! I'm on a bus and the driver is crazy!"

The bus driver stomped on the phone with his boot. Amber could not get past him. He was holding up both arms. She could not exit the bus now.

I should have got out when I had the chance, she decided. *But, every bus has an emergency exit!*

She turned and ran to the back of the bus. The driver followed her. Amber made it to the emergency back door and turned the door handle. She kicked back at the driver, and he stopped for a second. He was out of breath. "Don't run away from me," he said. "I'm not a fast runner."

Opening the door, Amber jumped down. Her ankle twisted and she fell on her knees. The driver took a slow step down. It was hard for him to move around. He was in very bad physical condition, but he looked at her and smiled.

He was in no hurry now.

Annex to Chapter 1

Summary

Amber is riding the city bus. It is late at night and she is the only passenger. The driver keeps looking at her. She does not recognize the road he is on. Amber asks what he is doing, and he begins to scare her. He stops the bus in an abandoned car park, and she escapes from the back door.

Multiple-choice questions
Select one answer for each question

1. Amber thinks the driver is weird because he:
   a. keeps looking at her
   b. keeps laughing
   c. smells bad
   d. all of the above

2. Amber stands up on the bus, but then almost falls. Why?
   a. She tripped on a bottle
   b. She was looking out a window
   c. The bus hits a hole in the road
   d. The driver is drinking and driving

3. Why does the driver breathe heavily?
   a. Because he is out of shape
   b. Because it is late at night
   c. Because he likes Amber's hair
   d. Because he is sick

4. Who does Amber call?
   a. Her brother

b. Her friends
c. The police
d. Her sister

5. What happens to Amber when she gets off the bus?
   a. The driver falls on her
   b. She hurts her ankle
   c. She runs to the police
   d. She makes a phone call

1. d
2. c
3. a
4. d
5. b

Chapter 2

Amber saw an old abandoned warehouse. The parking lot they were in was for the warehouse employees. But now, this business was gone. Closed forever. Most of the businesses in this part of town were closed. The buildings were not used by anyone. There weren't any houses around here either.

This was the emptiest part of town. Even if she screamed, no one would hear her.

"Why did you bring me out here?" she asked. She knew it was a dumb question, but she wanted to keep him talking. Perhaps she could talk him out of his plan. She could make him realize he was making a mistake. She could tell him that he didn't want to hurt her.

"You need more patience," the hairy driver said, walking toward her. His walk was funny. He walked more like a duck than a person. But, there was nothing funny about his behaviour. "Have patience," he said again. "You're going to learn why I brought you here. I will teach you. I'm going to teach you until you understand."

"You're crazy!" she yelled, talking a step back. "Somebody help me!"

"Love is crazy. And I'm in love with you!" He laughed again, then spit something on the ground. "By the way, you can yell and scream as much as you want to...but it won't do any good."

Amber turned in a circle, looking around her. She already knew he was right. No one could save her. She was alone.

Then, she saw something. Amber saw a small light in the darkness. There was only one tiny light coming from a small old building. The building was on a side street back behind the warehouse. Inside, a golden light was flickering.

Is that a candle? she wondered, since the light was not steady. It was flickering like a candle flame. *If there is a candle, then somebody must be inside! They would not leave a candle burning by itself.*

She ran in the direction of the flickering light. Her ankle was hurting her, but she had no choice. She had to take the pain. The man behind her was coming. He was not going to change his mind.

"Young lady, there is no reason to run away," he said. "You'll like me once you get to know me better."

"That's not going to happen!" she shouted. "Get away from me!"

"Where are you running to? There is nobody out here!"

She kept going even though her foot was hurting a lot. She was getting nearer to the building with the candlelight. It seemed like that was the only place to go.

It was hard to see. The night was darker than usual. There were clouds in the sky covering the stars. The moon was hiding behind the clouds too. But, Amber could see on top of the building. On the roof of the building was a cross.

Is that a church? Out here in the middle of nowhere?

She got closer and saw, yes, it was a church. The church looked abandoned too. Some of the windows were broken. Wooden boards were falling off the sides. The grass around the area was very tall.

No one had come here in many years.

If no one uses it, why is there a candle burning inside? I hope it isn't a homeless person living in there.

But, she changed her mind. Even if it was a homeless person, perhaps they could help her. Anything was better than fighting the crazy bus driver alone!

*

The front door was unlocked. Amber ran inside the empty church. She saw the candle in the window. There were candles in each of the windows, but there was nobody around.

She closed the door.

Oh no, there isn't a lock on it!

The bus driver was coming. He was walking fast, but he could not run. He was not in good enough shape for running. He was out of breath.

"I told you, don't make me chase you!" he said, looking through the window. His face was sweaty. He looked like an animal.

"Stop! Stop it! My sister will call the police. You heard me call her!"

"Yeah, but she doesn't know where you are."

"The police can track my phone."

The driver was holding her phone. He raised it. It was destroyed. "You should have held onto it better," he said, smiling his creepy smile. "Now stop running, little lady. You've got nowhere else to go."

Amber stood a step back. The driver was standing outside looking in the window. The door didn't have a lock on it. She needed to put something in front of the door to block him. There were a few heavy benches. She took one of the benches and started to drag it towards the door, but it was too late, he was coming in!

"Help!" she cried again. *Where was the preacher for this place? Someone had to be here because there were candles! They weren't burned down yet... Who had lit the candles?*

She tried to keep the door closed, but he was too heavy. He was pushing and pushing, and finally, he got inside. Amber punched at him with her fist, but she missed.

"Whoa, take it easy!" he said. "I don't want to fight you."

"You tricked me," she said. "This church...you live here, don't you? This is your place!"

"Are you kidding?" the bus driver said. He threw her phone over his shoulder. "I have a nice apartment. I would never live in a church. That is just weird."

"But you put the candles in here. It was a trick to get me to come inside."

"You're wrong about that first part. I did not put the candles here, but you're right about the second part. Yes, it was a trick..."

Then, Amber heard the sounds of the other person in the building. *Somebody else is here!*

The man walked out from behind a large curtain. He was very tall and skinny with long black hair. He wore an old black suit. At first, Amber thought maybe he was a preacher.

Like the bus driver, the man smelled terrible. He looked like he had not taken a shower in a long time, and he looked very hungry.

"Hi Fred," the fake preacher said to the bus driver. "Nice catch. You brought a good one tonight. But next time, bring me something to eat. You know I always like a good cheeseburger!"

"Stop complaining," the driver said. "And why did you call me Fred? Now she knows my name!"

"So? Who will she tell?"

Amber was trapped between them now. The driver was standing in front of the door, and the preacher was walking closer and closer.

"You're right," said Fred the bus driver. He looked at Amber with his red eyes. "The dead tell no secrets."

Annex to Chapter 2

Summary

Amber tries to escape the bus driver. She sees a building with a candle inside. When she runs to it, she sees it is an old church. She goes in, but there is no way to stop the driver. He comes inside too. Then, his friend comes out. They have Amber trapped!

Multiple-choice questions
Select one answer for each question

6. Why is the night darker than usual?
    a. Because it is so late
    b. Because of all the trees
    c. Because the sky is cloudy
    d. Because she is wearing sunglasses

7. Why can't Amber stop the driver from coming into the church?
    a. He comes through the window
    b. He breaks down the door
    c. She forgot to lock the door
    d. The door doesn't have a lock

8. What does the second man remind Amber of?
    a. A football player
    b. A bus driver
    c. A car salesman
    d. A preacher

9. What is the second man complaining?
    a. He is hungry

b. He is tired

c. He wants a drink

d. He wants more light

10. What does the bus driver do with Amber's phone?

    a. He leaves it on the bus

    b. He throws it outside

    c. He gives it to her

    d. He gives it to his friend

6. c
7. d
8. d
9. a
10. b

Chapter 3

Amber pleaded with the two men. "You don't have to do this," she said. "You can stop now. You can let me go!"

The fake preacher looked at his partner, Fred the bus driver. "You are very persuasive, young lady," he said. He smelled like a dirty toilet. He reached his hand into his pocket. Amber watched, wondering what he was going to do. He took out half of a cheese sandwich from his pocket and started eating it. "You think we should let you go?"

"Yes!"

"And you won't tell anybody?"

"No, I swear!" she said.

"You won't tell anyone what we tried to do?"

"If you let me go, I won't tell," Amber said. "But--have you two done this to other people? Have you done this before?"

Fred laughed and coughed. "Sometimes. A man needs a hobby, doesn't he?" He wiped sweat from his beard and took a step closer. "Listen honey, you aren't going to talk your way out of this. We won't let you go. So relax."

"Wait," the preacher said. "Let her finish talking. There is no rush. I like the sound of her voice."

"I like the sound of her screams," Fred said. "I don't care about the sound of her talking though."

Amber raised her hands. She was still holding her purse. "Guys, I want to give you every chance I can. I want you to realize that you have a choice. You can stop this at any time."

The preacher sat down on a bench. He crossed his legs and stared at her. He seemed very interested. "You want to give us 'every chance.' What do you mean? You have no power here. You are our prisoner."

"She just likes to talk," Fred said. "Tell her to be quiet. Let's get on with this!"

Amber ignored Fred. She sat down on the bench next to the preacher. "I'm saying, you two are adults. You have free choice. You can be criminals or you can act normal. You don't have to hurt people. You're right, I'm your prisoner. You're right, I have no power here. But, you do have power...the power to release me. Right now! And, you don't ever have to do this again."

"We like doing it," Fred said, crossing his arms. "And, if you don't shut up, I'm going to--"

"What? Kill me?" Amber asked. "I already know you're going to kill me. So, I have nothing to lose. Do I?"

"Oh, you have something to lose," Fred said. "And, you are going to lose it very soon."

"Then let me buy my way out," she said, opening her purse. "I have a thousand dollars in here. I'll give it to you if you let me go."

The preacher shook his head. "The money is already ours. Everything you have is ours."

"Darren, would you please stop talking to her?" Fred said.

"Oh, you didn't want me to call you Fred," the preacher said, standing up, "but now, you're saying my name!"

"Because you were right!" Fred said, taking a big breath. "What difference does it make, Darren? Who is she going to tell?"

"You're both right," Amber said. "I won't tell anyone and you won't either."

She took her small gun out of her purse and shot Darren, the fake preacher once. Calmly, she stood up from the bench. She pointed the gun at Fred who raised his hands in the air. Amber kept her eyes on him, then she pointed the gun back at Darren and shot him two more times. She wanted to make sure he was dead.

"Whoa! Don't kill me!" Fred said. "We were just messing around. We weren't really going to hurt you!"

"You said you've done this before?"

"No, I... I was lying. It wasn't true. I only said that to scare you."

"I gave you every chance to let me go, didn't I? Over and over, I kept saying you can stop," she said, pointing the gun at his stomach. "Things did not have to end like this. This didn't have to happen."

"I swear," Fred said, sweating again. He was trying to walk backward, but he hit a bench. "We weren't going to do anything to you. Our plan was to let you go."

"No it wasn't."

"It was! We weren't going to hurt you!"

"But I'm going to hurt you," she said, shooting him two times. Amber was an expert with guns. She knew exactly where to shoot someone if she wanted to kill them. She also knew where to shoot them, so they would not die.

Fred fell on the ground yelling and screaming. He was in pain, but he would not die, at least not for a few hours. Amber sat down and rested her injured foot.

"There is a little game I like to play with my sister," she explained. "We've been doing it for almost a year. We stay out late. We stay out until someone tries something stupid. Someone like you and the 'preacher' over there."

Her foot began to feel better, so she stood up. She picked up one of the burning candles.

"We let the stupid person or persons try to take us. Then, when they don't expect it, we kill them." She poured melted candle wax on Fred's beard. He yelled again.

"You tricked us!" he said.

"You tricked me first," she said. "I gave you the opportunity to stop. Do you want to give me the same chance? You want to give me a chance to stop?" She pointed the gun at his head. "I have one bullet left."

"Yes, yes! You can stop! You don't have to shoot me again!"

"Okay," she said, putting her gun back into her purse. "See? You convinced me. I won't shoot you again."

Amber held the candle to the man's pants. Fred's pants caught on fire. Then, she quickly ran out of the old church. She picked up her broken phone on the way out. Amber had another working phone in her bag, of course.

Aisha, Amber's twin sister, pulled her car up into the parking lot.

Right on time!

"Hi Sis," Aisha said, as Amber got into the car. "Looks like you won tonight."

The identical twin sisters sat in the car as the church caught fire.

"Thanks for playing 'Twin's Revenge,'" Amber said to the dead men in the church, smiling as her sister drove away.

Annex to Chapter 3

Summary

The preacher and the bus driver have Amber trapped in the church. She tries to talk them out of hurting her. She learns they have done this to others. They are not going to let her go... so she takes out a gun. She shots the preacher, then Fred. Fred realizes Amber had tricked them. Amber leaves the church; her sister picks her up in her car.

Multiple-choice questions
Select one answer for each question

11. What does the preacher keep in his pocket?
    a. A watch
    b. A sandwich
    c. French fries
    d. A phone

12. The preacher likes Amber's voice. What does Fred like?
    a. Her shoes
    b. Her purse
    c. Her screams
    d. Her attitude

13. Why does Amber keep talking?
    a. So they will think about what they are doing
    b. So they will get bored
    c. Because she is waiting on the police
    d. None of the above

14. How many shots does Amber fire in total?
    a. 3. 2 at Darren, 1 at Fred

    b. 4. 2 at Darren, 2 at Fred
    c. 5. 3 at Darren, 2 at Fred
    d. 6. 3 at Darren, 3 at Fred

15. How does Aisha know where to go?
    a. Amber told her during their call
    b. The police told her
    c. They knew about the church in advance
    d. Amber had a second phone in her purse

11. b
12. c
13. a
14. c
15. d

7. Discussions on Dating

Chapter 1

"I cannot go on a date with you," Dawn said on the phone. She was in northern California for the summer. College was over until next term. She was enjoying the long summer break, but she missed her friend, Dan. He had gone to Nevada to take college courses over the summer.

Dawn knew her friend liked her. He had liked her for a long time, but he had never had the courage to ask her out until now, over the phone.

"Yes, you can go on a date with me!" he said.

Dawn was twisting her long dark hair around her finger. She was lying on her bed in her bedroom. She was trying to think of an excuse to say. "My parents would kill me if I dated you!"

"Why?" Dan asked. He was in Nevada – several hours away by car. Dan was outside, sitting in a park. He had met Dawn's parents. He knew they did not like him.

He had a lot of tattoos and ear rings. His blonde hair was very spikey and his clothes were a little wild. Dawn's family was conservative. They didn't like "wild."

So, Dan knew the reason why. He didn't need her to answer his question. Instead, he asked, "Do you have to tell your parents?"

"Of course, I have to tell them. I don't keep secrets..."

"But, you are a grown woman."

"Look--you're a nice guy, Dan" Dawn said, but she didn't get to finish.

"I am!" Dan said, interrupting. "You're right, I really am a great guy. A terrific guy! Your parents would love me if they knew me better. They would adore me!"

"I'm sure they would like you eventually. Maybe not 'love' or 'adore.' But yes, sure, they would think you are boyfriend material."

"Or don't say anything to them. I'm sorry, Dawn, but you're being very old-fashioned..."

"What is wrong with that? I can't lie to my Mom and Dad," Dawn said, sitting up on her bed. "I won't."

"What, lying? Say nothing to them," Dan argued. He watched a woman jog by with her dog. "Don't tell them about me. That is not lying."

"Yes it is," she said. "It is a lie by omission."

"Oh, you are using the big words. 'Omission.' If you don't say anything, if you say nothing about me to them--"

"--then I have omitted the facts," Dawn said in a serious voice. But, she was only messing around. She was not really being very serious. "Anyways, omission is not a big word."

"I am failing my English class," Dan admitted. English was his second language. He was still learning. "So, it is a big word to me."

"If it is, then we're finished," she said, joking. "I cannot date someone with a small vocabulary."

"Ahh, but you would date me otherwise?"

Dawn laughed. "I guess you got me. Yes, I mean... I like you. There, I said it. Okay?"

"You said you like me," Dan replied. He had been sitting on a park bench. Now he stood up. "Great. But, that does nothing for me."

"What do you mean?" She had not expected him to say that.

"Think about it," he said. "Saying you like me makes it worse! Now I know you like me, so why can't we date? This is frustrating!"

"Let me finish," Dawn said. She got up from her bed. She was walking around the room. "I'm joking with you, Dan. I'll go out with you. When you are finished with your classes and you come back to California, we can see each other. But, I do have to tell my folks."

This was great news for Dan. His classes would be over next month, but he still wondered why she had to talk to her parents. It was very strange to him. "What do you need from them? You want to get their permission?"

"No, not their permission," she explained. "But it is our culture. You know, my family is not from America. We have different traditions where I am from."

"I know that. My family is the same."

"Yes, we came from another country. Where we come from, we respect our parents. We include our mothers and fathers in our daily lives."

"That isn't fair to say that. I respect my parents too!"

"You do? Do you include them in your daily life, Dan?"

"Well," Dan said, thinking. He did not really see them very often. He was away from home and did not go visit them very often. And, he did not ask their advice about things, but Dan did not want to tell Dawn any of that. "I try to call them every week," he said.

"That is not the same thing, but it does not matter. When will you be done with your summer term at college?"

"It is over next month. This is a very short term, you know. I am only taking these classes to make up for last term. I did not do well in class last term."

"Yes, I heard about that. You failed two classes," Dawn said. "But, I know you are very smart. You can do it!"

"Thanks," he said. "I do study a lot. In fact, my teachers know that I am a good student, but the classes are all in English. That is why I have trouble sometimes."

Dawn nodded. She understood completely. She had also had trouble last year in college, then she hired a professional tutor. The tutor helped her a lot. "When you come back, I'm going to help you study English," she said. "I will show you everything my tutor taught me."

"Really? That will help me a lot!" Dan said. "But, I need to do something first."

"What is that?"

"Before you can be my tutor," he said, smiling, "I will need to ask my parents."

"Very funny," Dawn said. "Just for that, I am going to be a very tough tutor!"

Annex to Chapter 1

Summary

Dawn lives in California. Her friend, Dan, has gone to Nevada. He is taking college courses over the summer. He calls her because he wants to go out with her. She tells him she will need to talk with her parents. He thinks she is being very old-fashioned, but Dawn agrees to see Dan when he returns. She also offers to help him with his English.

Multiple-choice questions
Select one answer for each question

1. How far away from Dawn is Dan, if driving a car?
   a. Two hours away
   b. Several hours away
   c. Twenty-four hours away
   d. One day away

2. What reason does Dan give for failing two classes?
   a. The classes were in English
   b. The classes were in German
   c. The classes were science and technology
   d. The classes were boring

3. Why does Dawn insist on telling her parents about Dan?
   a. She needs their permission
   b. She is not allowed to date yet
   c. She wants them to give her money
   d. She likes to include them in her life

4. Dan thinks her parents do not like him. Why?

a. Because they are a different religion
b. Because they have different ethnic backgrounds
c. Because they are conservative and he looks too "wild"
d. Because he is conservative and they look too "wild"

5. Dawn agrees to go on a date with Dan when:
    a. She turns 21 years old
    b. He asks to marry her
    c. He returns from Nevada
    d. He combs his hair differently

1. b
2. a
3. d
4. c
5. c

Chapter 2

Caprice loved talking on the telephone. She enjoyed chatting with her friends... especially about their boyfriends! It was a rainy day outside, and she was bored. She decided to call her old friend Dawn. She had heard a rumour and wanted to learn the truth.

"So, Dawn," she said, "Did you know Jack is in Nevada now?"

"Really?" Dawn said. "I remember your boyfriend Jack! He's cute. Very handsome. What's he doing out there in Nevada?"

"He's talking summer classes. In fact, you'll never guess where."

"You're right," Dawn said. She hated guessing games. Besides, she was in a hurry. It was almost time to start work. She was putting her clothes out on the bed. She was not really paying attention. "Nevada is a big state. I do not know where Jack could be."

"Jack is at the same college as Dan!"

"Oh. That's interesting," Dawn said. She was not sure why Caprice was telling her this. "I'm sure Jack and Dan will be glad to hang out together. Do they know each other very well?"

Caprice smiled. "They know each other a little. They are becoming friends. In fact, they have been talking a lot lately. So, Dawn... Dan told Jack that you two are dating!"

Oh, so that's what this call is about, Dawn thought.

"Well... I would not say we are dating. But, I told him we could date. When he returns to California."

"Come on, don't be shy. I'm your friend. Tell me everything. You know, I used to date Dan. We dated two years ago when we were freshmen in college."

"I remember that," Dawn said. She remembered, but not very well. Caprice dated a lot.

"So, did you think you could keep this a secret from me?"

Dawn was getting ready for work. She looked at her clock. There were only twenty minutes to get dressed and get to her job. She did not have a lot of time to talk. "There isn't much to tell, Caprice. And, I'm in a little bit of a hurry."

"Just give me the main details then."

"Okay, fine. You are very persistent! Dan asked me to date him, but he didn't ask when he was here. He waited until he had gone to Nevada!"

"Men. They have very bad timing, don't they? I remember Dan was always late for things."

Dawn wanted to switch the subject. She did not want to think about Dan and Caprice as a couple. "What about you and Jack? Jack is so nice! You guys were seeing each other a long time. Are you two still a couple?"

"Not really," Caprice said. She had not told anyone this before. "Actually, we broke up before he left for Nevada."

"Oh, I didn't know that! You never told me. I'm sorry. So, you do not see him anymore?"

"We broke up on good terms. We are still friends. But--how can I say this? Jack was not a good boyfriend."

Dawn knew her friend was very picky about her boyfriends. That is why there had been so many of them. Caprice usually only dated a person a few times, but she had stayed with Jack for a few months. Everyone thought they were a nice couple. In fact, Dawn thought Jack might even be the big one!

She was shocked to hear anything negative about Jack. "Not a good boyfriend? Why? What did he do?" She checked her clock again. She was running out of time, but she wanted to hear this, so she put the phone on speakerphone. She was able to dress while talking and listening.

Caprice said, "For starters--Jack likes to flirt with other women."

"Oh, no. Are you serious? Was he... was he cheating on you?"

"I don't think so. No. I am sure he was not seeing anyone else, but I do not like my boyfriends to even look at someone else."

Dawn shrugged her shoulders. "Boys will be boys. Looking isn't touching. I mean, looking does not mean anything. You never looked at somebody else?"

"Maybe I did, but Jack was not just looking, he was talking to them too. He was flirting with them."

"Where?"

"What?"

"Where was he talking to other women?" Dawn asked.

"At the nightclub."

"Where he works?"

"Yes. He still works at Zara's, my mom's nightclub. He is a bartender. He serves drinks to pretty girls all night long."

Dawn laughed, then covered her mouth.

"What's so funny?" Caprice asked. She was getting a little angry.

"Sorry. Didn't you help him get that job?"

Caprice did not like to be reminded about that. "Yeah. I did help him get the job. If I could go back in time, I would stop myself."

"Well Caprice, be fair. If Jack is a bartender, then it is his job to talk to customers."

"I guess so."

"You guess so? Come on, be reasonable! You are not being fair. I mean, if he is talking to people at the club..."

"He's flirting with them. He is not just talking. There is a big difference! Don't be naïve."

"I'm not naïve. You're being too picky. Maybe he is only speaking that way for tips. You know, he gets more money if he is extra nice. There is no reason to be jealous. He is only talking to be nice."

"He does not have to be *that* nice. Besides, you would not like it if Dan was acting that way. You would be jealous, wouldn't you?"

"No. Maybe I would not care. Right now, it does not matter. I am not yet dating Dan."

"Hmmm. That's true. You are single. So, if you are going to take Jack's side, then you date him! And, I'll take Dan!"

"What? Are you crazy?" Dawn asked. She did not have any time left. "Look, I have to go to work. I know you are joking, but that isn't funny."

"You said you do not get jealous. What's the problem?" Caprice asked.

Dawn sighed. She grabbed something to eat from her kitchen. She was going to have to eat at work. "We can have this conversation later. I do not have time to argue." She hung up the phone without saying goodbye to her friend.

Annex to Chapter 2

Summary

Caprice calls her friend Dawn. She heard that Dan asked Dawn out on a date. They talk about boyfriends. Caprice says she broke up with her old boyfriend, Jack. She says Jack was flirting with other women. Dawn defends Jack and says Caprice is being too picky. They argue a little, but Dawn has to go to work. Caprice offers to date Dan, and let Dawn date Jack.

Multiple-choice questions
Select one answer for each question

6. Why was Caprice bored?
   a. Because she did not have to work
   b. Because it was raining outside
   c. Because the electricity went off
   d. Because she broke up with her boyfriend

7. Who told Caprice that Dan asked Dawn on a date?
   a. Jack told her
   b. Zara told her
   c. Dan told her
   d. None of the above

8. Why does Caprice date a lot?
   a. Because she is bored
   b. Because she is picky
   c. Because she enjoys dating different people
   d. Because she is looking for a husband

9. Why does Dawn think Caprice is a jealous person?

a. Because Caprice thinks all men cheat
b. Because Caprice thinks Jack was cheating
c. Because Caprice thinks Jack was flirting
d. Because Dawn does not like Caprice anymore

10. What is Caprice's suggestion at the end of the story?
    a. She thinks Dawn and Dan should break up
    b. She thinks she should get back together with Jack
    c. She thinks Dawn should not date anyone
    d. She thinks Dawn should date Jack

6. b
7. a
8. b
9. c
10. d

Chapter 3

Dan was very excited. His summer college courses were almost over. He was doing well in the courses. He would get good grades.

Good grades will help my grade point average, he thought. *When I go back to my university in California, maybe I will get a scholarship.*

He was glad to be leaving Nevada soon. In two weeks, he would be home. He could see Dawn again. She had promised to go on a date with him when he returned.

They had known each other a long time, but he had never had the courage to ask her out. It had been easier to ask over the phone. It was easier to ask when he was not there.

In some ways, it did not seem real. Dating Dawn had been his dream...

Soon, that dream is going to come true!

His phone rang. It was his friend Jack. He had known Jack for a long time, but they had never been close friends. Now, they were going to the same summer school. Now, they were becoming good friends. Sometimes, they ate lunch together. At night, they liked to watch movies together, when their studies were over.

But, Dan had always noticed that Jack was a little sad. Something was always bothering Jack. And now, Dan knew what it was...

"Hi, Jack," he said, answering the phone.

"Dan! Hey, I need to talk to you."

"That's funny. I wanted to talk to you too."

"Oh," Jack said, a little surprised. "Alright, you can go first. What's going on?"

"Dawn told me you are not seeing Caprice anymore."

Jack was surprised again. He and Caprice had not made their break up public. "That's true," Jack admitted. "I didn't want to say anything. I was hoping Caprice and I would get back together."

"That is what I wanted to talk about," Dan said. "I could tell something has been bothering you, but I did not know what. I was worried about you."

"Thanks, man. I'm okay though. Really."

"Are you sure?" Dan asked. "Do you want to talk about what happened?"

"Oh, you know how women are," Jack said. He laughed, even though he did not think it was funny. He was still friends with Caprice, but his feelings were very hurt. He did not think she had been fair to him. "She thought I was flirting with other women. She accused me of trying to attract a new girlfriend."

"Really? I have not known you very long," Dan said. "I mean, I did not know you very well, but I do now. You are a nice guy. That does not sound like you!"

"It isn't," Jack agreed. It felt good to have someone to talk to. "I never did that! But, Caprice thinks I did. I cannot change her mind. She thinks I flirted with my customers."

"But you didn't?"

"I did a *little,* but it was not really flirting, just being extra nice. You know what I mean? It was totally innocent."

Dan asked, "What do you mean?"

"I only did it to get bigger tips," Jack said. "That is how those types of jobs work. You don't get paid very much, so you have to work for tips!"

Dan nodded. "I understand. I worked as a waiter in a restaurant. My salary was very low, but I was friendly. The customers loved me, so I made better tips than the others."

"Yes, that is exactly right!" Jack said. "It is simple. Why can't Caprice understand that? Hey, maybe you could talk to her."

Dan thought about that. "I don't think that is a good idea, Jack."

"Why not?"

"I have to tell you something. It is not a big deal, but you should know. I dated Caprice for a little while; not very long, and it was a long time ago."

"Yes, I know," Jack said. "So what?"

"Well... Caprice is awesome," Dan said. "She is great. I will be honest, I liked her a lot back then, but actually, she was jealous of me too."

"What? She thought you were flirting with others?" Jack couldn't believe it. He was not the first guy to deal with this problem.

"That's right. It sounds like you are having the same issue I had."

Jack was glad to be able to talk about these things. It was a relief. He had been quiet about his feelings... but now, he talked!

But, Jack had forgotten--he wanted to ask Dan something too!

"Dan, I have a question. I started talking about my problems, and I forgot to ask you."

"That's okay. What's up?"

"It's about Dawn. You mentioned you were going to start dating her?"

"Yes. I have wanted to go out with her for a long time, but I was always too shy. I never asked her out, but finally, I did!"

"And she said yes?"

Dan paused. Why was he asking about Dawn suddenly? "Yes. She wanted to talk to her parents first. That's what she said. But--"

"Why does she want to do that?"

"I don't know. She said she likes to keep them involved in her life."

"Doesn't that sound strange to you?"

"No. Maybe a little bit. Why are you asking this, Jack?"

"I was just curious," Jack said. "Because she's..."

"She's what?"

"You know she comes to Zara's sometimes. The bar I work at?"

Dan didn't know that, but it did not matter to him. Lots of people go to the nightclub. "Why do I need to know about that?"

"Because she is one of my customers. I need to tell you something, Dan. I think Dawn is very cute. Sometimes, I talk to her when she comes to the club. I was thinking about asking her on a date."

"What?" Dan asked. He couldn't believe it! "Are you serious?"

"Listen to me. I'm not going to do it. I won't ask her out since she said yes to you, but I wanted to make sure. I don't have a girlfriend. Caprice broke up with me, so you know... I thought about Dawn."

"Sorry, man. I got to her before you did! You will have to work things out with Caprice!"

Annex to Chapter 3

Summary

Dan and Jack have become friends. Jack calls Dan to talk. Dan has been worried about Jack, and he learns that Jack broke up with his girlfriend. Jack says Caprice thought he had been flirting with other women. Then, Jack mentions that he considered asking Dawn on a date, but he changed his mind, he learned Dan had already asked Dawn out.

Multiple-choice questions
Select one answer for each question

11. Why does Dan need good grades?
    a. He wants a college scholarship
    b. His parents are angry
    c. The college was going to ask him to leave
    d. To make Dawn happy

12. What had Dan noticed about Jack?
    a. That Jack likes to flirt
    b. That Jack likes to eat a lot
    c. That Jack seems sad
    d. That Jack gets good grades

13. Why does Jack say he is extra nice to customers?
    a. Because he wants to date them
    b. Because he wants tips
    c. Because it is part of his job
    d. Because he is a very friendly person

14. Why can Dan understand Jack's reason for being extra nice to customers?

a. Because Dan watched Jack at work
b. Because Dan is Jack's friend
c. Because Dan worked as a waiter and also got tips
d. Because Dan worked as a bartender and also got tips

15. Who does Jack say is one of his customers at the nightclub?
    a. Caprice
    b. Zara
    c. Dawn's parents
    d. Dawn

11. a
12. c
13. b
14. c
15. d

8. Monster Challenge

Chapter 1

"Is your job boring?" asked the hairy green creature on the television.

"No," Wagner the Werewolf said, talking to the TV. He finished his drink and crushed the can in his hand.

"Do you get tired of scaring people all day?" the advertisement continued. "Would you like to try something new? What about a job where you can be nice to people instead?"

"No thanks," Wagner said, switching the channel. "What is the point of being a monster," he asked, "if you don't scare people? And sometimes, eat them."

He had never liked commercials. He would rather watch ice skating than commercials. Of course, most werewolves did not have very much patience. He threw the crushed can into a trash can.

"I agree!" said a voice with no body.

"Who said that?" Wagner asked. The room was very dark, except for the light from the television. He did not see anyone else, so he smelled the air. He recognized the scent immediately. "Oh, it's *you*. I didn't know you were coming tonight."

Doctor Griffin, the "Invisible Man" nodded his head, but Wagner could not see it. The Werewolf could, of course, smell the human. Werewolves have very good noses, and humans have very bad smells.

"I can never fool you," Griffin said with a laugh. He was in a happy mood. He sat down in an empty chair and picked up a newspaper. The only thing the Werewolf could see was a pair of shorts and the newspaper. The Invisible Man did not like to wear a lot of clothes. He preferred to sneak around, so no one could see him.

They were at Count Dracula's new mansion in Virginia. It was very large and expensive. It was surrounded by a small forest. There were a lot of woods and hills in Virginia. It was a good place for monsters to live and hunt.

They were waiting for Dracula to come home. He was their boss and tonight was the monthly meeting. Everyone had to come. Attendance was mandatory for all the "classic" monsters, even if you had to come from overseas.

"Anyway, I agree with you, Wagner," Griffin said. "If you are going to be a monster, you might as well scare people." He turned the page of his newspaper, but he was secretly looking at the Werewolf.

Wagner frowned and showed his sharp teeth. "But, you are not really a monster," he said. "You are just a human that no one can see. That does not make you a monster."

"I think it depends on your definition of 'monster.'"

"Okay. By my definition, you are not a monster. Where is Frankenstein's creature? Take a look at that big ugly guy. That is a monster!"

"Be quiet," Griffin said, "Keep your voice down. I think he is in the house!"

"So? His hearing is terrible."

"Well, I cannot argue with you. Old Franky is one of the world's most horrible monsters," the Invisible Man agreed. "I cannot compare to him. He is much more horrible and scary than I am."

"You are not scary at all," the Werewolf interrupted.

"But," Griffin said, ignoring the insult, "Frankenstein's creature is so stupid! He can never be a leader. Do you know what I mean? He does not have much potential."

"You don't know him very well. He is smarter than he looks. Besides, no one said you must be intelligent to be a monster."

"I realize that," Griffin said. "But, to make a real impact on the world, you have to be smart. Look at me, I'm a doctor!"

"Ohh, a doctor! Big deal. I guess if you want to be a boss, you should be smart," Wagner said. "But, most of us are not interested in power. In fact, most of us are happy staying hidden. We don't need a lot of attention. We don't need to 'be important.' We scare a random person once a month, or eat somebody once in a while, but we are not hungry for power. You should know that by now."

"I think that is the problem," Griffin said. "We need to be better organized. We need to be smarter, then we could take over the world!"

The Werewolf yawned. The Invisible Man was not paying attention. He always talked about the same things, and Wagner had heard this speech before. The Invisible Man was only interested in taking over the world. It was his obsession.

Wagner walked into the kitchen to make microwave popcorn. "If you want to rule the planet, go ahead!" he shouted from the kitchen. "Nobody is stopping you!"

"I cannot do it by myself. I need the other monsters. We have to work together as a team!"

"Most of the others do not care about that stuff," Wagner said. He walked back into the living room a few minutes later. He was carrying a bowl of popcorn.

The Werewolf changed the channel again. There was nothing good on. He turned the television off and stood up. With the TV off, the room was completely black.

"Hey, it is too dark in here," Griffith complained. "I can't see in the dark!"

"I can," Wagner said. He walked behind the Invisible Man's chair. He grabbed the newspaper and tore it apart.

"Arrgh!" Griffin yelled.

"So," the Werewolf said, "now you know what it is like when you can't see somebody. It is annoying, isn't it?"

"I can't help being invisible," Griffin said. "I didn't ask to be this way!"

"Yes you did! You made the potion which turned you invisible!"

"Well...," Griffin said, tripping over a small table. "Turn a light on, please!"

Somewhere in the darkness outside, a dog howled. A door opened and a breeze of air came into the room. Dracula walked in without making a sound. "Good evening," he said. He flipped on a light switch with a long finger. "What are you two talking about?"

"We are talking about monsters being dumb," said the Invisible Man.

"I see," Dracula said. "I hope you are not referring to me." The old vampire looked directly at Griffin.

Annex to Chapter 1

Summary

It is time for the monthly Monster Meet-Up. Wagner, the Werewolf, and Griffin, the Invisible Man, are at Dracula's mansion in Virginia. They are arguing about monsters being stupid. Griffin thinks monsters should take over the world. Dracula comes home and wants to know what they are talking about.

Multiple-choice questions
Select one answer for each question

1. What is Griffin wearing?
   a. Nothing
   b. A suit
   c. Shorts
   d. Pajamas

2. How does Wagner know it is Griffin?
   a. He recognizes the smell
   b. He can see in the dark
   c. He can see invisible people
   d. He recognizes the voice

3. Who do they think is the most horrible monster?
   a. Dracula
   b. The Werewolf
   c. Swamp Creature
   d. Frankenstein's creature

4. What is nice about Dracula's mansion?

a. It has a large kitchen
b. It is surrounded by a small forest
c. It has five restrooms
d. It has a swimming pool

5. What is Griffin obsessed with?
   a. Popcorn
   b. Not wearing clothes
   c. Taking over the world
   d. Television

1. c
2. a
3. d
4. b
5. c

Chapter 2

Somehow, Dracula could always tell where the Invisible Man was. Vampires had many secret powers. Since Dracula was the oldest vampire, he had many abilities. He never let anyone know everything he could do. He liked to be mysterious.

"I didn't mean you, boss," said Griffin. "Actually, Wagner is the one who brought it up. He said most monsters are stupid."

Dracula smiled. His red lips were very dark, compared to his pale white face. "Of course, monsters are stupid, but they are smarter than the humans."

The Invisible Man knew it was an insult. He would always be a human, even if other humans could not see him, but he was so different from other people. Most of the time, he *felt* like a monster, even if he was not one. That is why he wanted to work with the monsters. He needed them to do what he wanted...

"Mister Hyde is a smart fellow," the Werewolf said as he picked up his bowl of popcorn. "But, I think the average monster is a complete idiot. We really need a better education system, Dracula."

No one ever talked to Dracula like that, except Wagner. Most of the others were afraid of the old vampire. There was good reason to be afraid of him, but the vampire and the werewolf were friends. Sometimes, they even went hunting together.

"We do not need smarter monsters. We have a few bright ones," Dracula stated. "Mister Hyde, you, myself--I am probably the brightest one."

"You are, boss," the Invisible Man said. He gave a thumbs-up, but no one saw it.

But, Wagner was very powerful and bold. He challenged the old vampire. "Are you sure you are the smartest of us all?" he asked.

"Who is brighter than I am? Tell me the name of a smarter monster! You can't!"

"I'm thinking," the Werewolf said, chewing a mouthful of popcorn. He licked the salt off of his long fingernails. "What about that guy in the bandages?"

"What guy in bandages?" the Invisible Man asked. "You mean the wrapped up guy?"

"Yes, he's all wrapped in bandages--"

Dracula laughed and the ground shook. "You don't mean the Mummy? Are you kidding me? He is a total idiot!"

The Werewolf's eyes glowed bright red. "The Mummy is dumb now, but he was not always like that. Before he died, he was the ruler of Egypt! He was a smart person back in the old days."

"That is only a rumour," Dracula said, rolling his eyes. "Anyone can say 'I was the ruler of Egypt.' Whatever! He has never been able to prove anything."

Wagner scratched his back. "Why would he lie about it?"

"He is crazy! Last month, he said he won the Olympic Gold Medal for swimming!"

The Invisible Man coughed. "I remember that." He tried to sneak his hand into the bowl of popcorn, but the Werewolf caught it.

"Don't touch my popcorn. Get your own!"

Suddenly, another person entered the room. Actually, it was not a person, it was the Swamp Creature. "It's true!" said the Swamp Creature. Most of the others had a hard time understanding it. It did not speak the English language very well. It had a large mouth like a fish, and it did not like being out of the water. Most of the time, it lived underwater, but tonight, it had come for the monthly Monster Meet-Up. "It's true," the Swamp Creature repeated. "The Mummy was an Egyptian Pharaoh thousands of years ago!"

"I doubt it," Dracula said. "But, it does not matter. He was not a monster back in those days. That is what we are talking about. The Mummy became a monster later, after he died and came back."

"How did he do that?" asked the Invisible Man. "I would like to come back from the dead."

"I can help you with that," Dracula said, stepping closer.

"Wait! I don't want to come back as a vampire!"

"You would rather come back as a mindless mummy?"

"No...but I don't want to drink blood."

"Have you ever tried it?"

"No! That is disgusting..."

Dracula gave him an evil stare.

"I mean, um... I'm sure it is not that bad. But," Griffin said to his boss, "you were a human once, right, Count Dracula?"

"All vampires begin as humans, then we become vampires."

"By dying?

"It is complicated, but yes."

"Then you are like the Mummy!" the Invisible Man said. It was a mistake.

Dracula flew across the room and grabbed Griffin by his invisible neck. "Do not compare me to him!"

"Wait, wait... are you going to kill me?"

"I'm thinking about it," Dracula said. "Probably."

"Don't make me a vampire. I want to stay human."

"Why?" Wagner asked, spitting out a popcorn kernel. "You always say you want to be a monster!"

"I want to stay human," Griffin repeated. "Because I don't want to become stupid. I may not be the smartest person on Earth--"

"You are the dumbest!" Dracula said, bringing his sharp teeth close to Griffin's face.

"--but even the dumbest human is smarter than the smartest monster!"

Dracula was so angry he threw Griffin across the room. No one else could see the Invisible Man, but they saw a window break. Dracula had thrown Griffin through the window. He had fallen into a bushy shrub outside.

Griffin stood up. He looked in the window. "I'm okay! And I challenge you, Dracula, to a contest!"

"I can't believe it," the Werewolf said. "Never pick a fight with the King of the Vampires!"

"I'll tear you apart!" Dracula shouted.

"No, not a fight," the Invisible Man said. "You say you are the smartest monster. You say I am the dumbest human. Let's see if the dumbest human is smarter than the smartest monster! That is my challenge!"

The other monsters looked at their boss. Dracula had no choice. He accepted the challenge.

Summary

Griffin compares Dracula to the Mummy. Dracula does not like the Mummy, so he gets angry and throws Griffin out a window. Griffin is alright; he gets up and he challenges Dracula to a contest. He does not want to fight, but he wants to see who is smarter--a monster or a human! Dracula agrees to the contest.

Multiple-choice questions
Select one answer for each question

6. Why is Wagner able to say what he wants to Dracula?
    a. Because he is stronger than Dracula
    b. Because he is friends with Dracula
    c. Because he is older than Dracula
    d. Because he is smarter than Dracula

7. Which country was the Mummy ruler of?
    a. Virginia
    b. Transylvania
    c. Egypt
    d. Germany

8. Why doesn't Griffin want Dracula to turn him into a vampire?
    a. He doesn't want to drink blood
    b. He is afraid of dying
    c. He doesn't like vampires
    d. He thinks he will become stupid

9. Which one of them does not like the Mummy?

a. Swamp Creature
b. Wagner
c. Griffin
d. Dracula

10. Why does Griffin challenge Dracula?
    a. He thinks he is smarter than Dracula
    b. He thinks he is stronger than Dracula
    c. He wants Dracula to kill him
    d. He wants Wagner to kill Dracula

6. b
7. c
8. a
9. d
10. a

Chapter 3

Griffin explained the rules of his challenge at the Monster Meet-Up. He wanted to be the next leader of the monsters. This was his big chance!

"Who is the most powerful of the monsters? We know it is Count Dracula, our leader!" he said. The others sat in the living room, listening. Frankenstein's creature had finally arrived, and a few zombies were sitting on the floor like children. There was also a witch from the East, Mister Hyde (who had flown in from England), and the ancient Mummy. The Mummy was too stiff to sit down, so he stood in the corner. He stood away from the fireplace.

"And, who is the smartest of the monsters?" The Invisible Man waited for anyone to answer.

"Dracula is," Dracula said. "Stop wasting our time. What is your point Doctor Griffin?"

"Yes, you are the smartest," Griffin agreed. "Dracula is the smartest monster. And, what has he done for us?"

The others looked around. Dracula crossed his arms, but said nothing.

"Anybody?" Griffin asked. "Let me ask again--if he is the best we have, what do we have to show for it? Nothing! After all these years, we continue to hide in the shadows. We act like we are afraid of the humans. We should be in charge of them!"

"We have our own television channel," the Swamp Creature said. The others nodded.

"It is terrible!" Griffin said. "All it plays are old reruns of shows. That is not important!"

"What is your point?" Wagner said. He was curious to hear about the challenge.

"You all have allowed me to be part of the monster team. Even though I am a human, you let me act like a monster. Thank you for that. But now, let me help you! You are my brothers and sisters. I can do better for you than Dracula has done. He was a human, years and years ago, but he has forgot about human greed and human ambition. He is lazy!"

Dracula's eyes glowed. He chewed on his lip. He really wanted to kill Griffin, but he waited. He also wanted to hear about the challenge.

Griffin could tell the others were getting restless, so he made his announcement to them. "I challenge Dracula for leadership of the monsters. Here is what I need from you all. You will build two traps. Build both traps exactly the same. Make them identical. There can be only one way to escape the traps. I will not know it, and he will not know it. Do not tell us how to escape."

"That's it?" Wagner asked. "That sounds simple enough." The Werewolf looked around the room. "What do you all say? Do you agree with this plan?"

The monsters loved traps. Some of them were very good at making traps. They laughed and grunted and clapped. They agreed to the Invisible Man's plan. Wagner nodded his hairy head and turned to his boss. "What do you say, Count Dracula?"

"I am smarter than that idiot," he said, pointing at the Invisible Man. "Any trap they build, I will escape from in seconds. But, you must not use any garlic or crosses," he said. "That would not be fair. The humans do not mind those things, but I hate garlic, and I really hate crosses!"

"Then we are all agreed," Griffin stated. "How long will it take to build the traps?"

*

Zara, the witch from the East, called her friends. They flew to Virginia on their broomsticks. Witches were great trap builders. "Remember, no magic! And no garlic or crosses either," said Zara. They built two giant black boxes. Each black box was made of heavy metal. There were no doors or windows. There was only a small hole left open. The hole was big enough for a person to climb inside. Once the person was in, the witches would close the hole up. They would use metal torches, which were hot enough to melt the heavy metal. It would be as if there had never been any opening. The boxes would have no way out.

"Tell Count Dracula the traps are ready!"

*

Dracula was impressed. The witches were fast workers. They had built their traps in less than one week. They placed the traps near the edge of Foggy Bottom Swamp.

"Very nice work, ladies," Dracula said. He looked around the swamp. It was very dark. The other monsters had all gathered together to watch the contest. The moon was full and bright, and it was very late at night. The contest would begin at midnight.

"Where is Griffin?" Mister Hyde asked. "Did he get scared?"

Wagner smelled the air. "No, he is here. I can smell his stinky clothes."

Griffin, the Invisible Man, stepped out from his hiding place. He was wearing clothes and his face was wrapped in white bandages. He also wore dark glasses. Everyone could easily see him. "Sorry I am late," he said quietly. He walked forward, toward the black boxes. "There is no reason to delay. Let us begin!"

Griffin climbed into the first box. The others watched Dracula. Dracula shrugged his shoulders and got into the second box.

"Seal them up," Wagner said. The witches used their torches and sealed up the holes. When the holes were sealed, the Werewolf nodded. "Now, Swamp Creature! Push the boxes into the swamp!"

"I did not know that was part of the plan!" Mister Hyde said.

Wagner stared at him. "It is now. Do it, Swamp Creature!"

Swamp Creature was incredibly strong. He easily pushed both the heavy boxes into the water. They sank to the bottom of the water. No bubbles of air came up. There were no holes in the boxes.

"Now what?" Mister Hyde asked.

"Now we wait," Wagner said. They sat and waited... and waited. They waited all night, but neither Dracula nor Griffin ever escaped their boxes.

"What do we do now?" Zara asked.

"I think we should celebrate," said a voice from the woods. "We have a winner!" Griffin jumped down from a tree. He was wearing a white bed sheet. "Boo!" he said.

The other monsters jumped and yelled. Wagner, the Werewolf, grinned. "So...how did you escape?"

"I did not escape. I never went inside the box," Griffin explained.

"What? Then who went inside?"

"That idiot, the Mummy! I tricked him. I dressed him up like me, and I put a speaker in his pocket," Griffin said, holding up a tiny microphone. "You heard my voice, but it sounded like it came from him."

Wagner laughed and clapped Griffin on the back. "Dracula will be very angry when he escapes."

The witches looked at each other. "What do you mean, when he escapes? The boxes are sealed. There is no way to escape them."

Wagner's eyes got wide. He slapped his forehead. "You were supposed to make a way to escape the traps! Oh, you stupid monsters!"

"See, I told you they are all too dumb," Griffin said.

"Then you are correct," Wagner said. "We do have a winner! I was wrong about you, Griffin. You *are* a monster. The worst kind of monster!"

"The human kind," Griffin said, laughing. "And now, let's talk about taking over the world..."

Annex to Chapter 3

Summary

Griffin tells about his challenge. He wants the monsters to build two traps. He will go in one, Dracula will go in the other. They build two boxes. When Griffin and Dracula go inside, Swamp Creature pushes the boxes into the swamp, then Griffin comes out of a tree he was hiding in. He explains that he tricked the Mummy into going inside the box. Then, Wagner realizes the witches did not make the traps escapable. Griffin wins the contest!

Multiple-choice questions
Select one answer for each question

11. Why do the monsters like Griffin's challenge idea?
    a. Because they think he will die
    b. Because they think Dracula will die
    c. Because they like traps
    d. Because they like swamps

12. Dracula agrees as long as they do not use:
    a. garlic and clover
    b. crosses and chalk
    c. garlic and swamp water
    d. crosses and garlic

13. The boxes are black and made of:
    a. wood
    b. concrete
    c. straw
    d. metal

14. What does Griffin use to make his voice come from the Mummy?
    a. A recording
    b. A microphone and speaker
    c. A microphone and radio
    d. A speakerphone

15. How will Dracula and the Mummy escape?
    a. They can't
    b. They will wait until the sun comes out
    c. They will swim out
    d. They will use the doors on the boxes

11. c
12. d
13. d
14. b
15. a

THE END

This title is also available as an audiobook.

For more information, please visit the Amazon store.

Thank You For Reading!

I hope you have enjoyed these stories, and that your English has improved as a result! A lot of hard work went into creating this book, and if you would like to support me, the best way to do so would be with an honest review on the Amazon store. This helps other people find the book, and lets them know what to expect.

      To do this:

1. Visit http://www.amazon.com
2. Click "Your Account" in the menu bar.
3. Click "Your Orders" from the drop-down menu.
4. Select this book from the list and leave an honest review!

Thank you for your support,

- Olly Richards

More from Olly

If you have enjoyed this book, you will love all the other free language learning content that I publish each week on my blog and podcast: *I Will Teach You A Language.*

The *I Will Teach You A Language* Blog
Study hacks and mind tools for independent language learners.
http://iwillteachyoualanguage.com

The *I Will Teach You A Language* Podcast
I answer your language learning questions twice a week on the podcast.
http://iwillteachyoualanguage.com/itunes

Here is where I hang out on social media. Why not come and say hi?

Facebook:
http://facebook.com/iwillteachyoualanguage

Twitter:
http://twitter.com/olly_iwtyal